ENGLISH MADE EASIER

Joseph Bellafiore

Author of
Words at Work
Adventures With Words—Book 1
Adventures With Words—Book 2
English Language Arts
Essentials of English

Dedicated to serving

AMSCO

our nation's youth

When ordering this book, please specify:
either R 150 P or ENGLISH MADE EASIER, paperback

AMSCO SCHOOL PUBLICATIONS, INC.
315 Hudson Street   New York, N.Y. 10013

To LOUIS

ISBN 0-87720-342-3

TO THE STUDENT

Dear Student,

Hello! Let's get acquainted through this letter. I wrote this book to show you how to handle English better in your everyday use of language.

Everything you need to know about grammar, sentences, spelling, punctuation, and vocabulary is made easier here. You will find the "workshop" idea in every topic. For example, there is a clear explanation for each part of speech, some illustrations, a series of exercises, and a review test. At the end of each topic, there is a short summary box headed "In This Lesson We Learned." Memorize the few important rules as you go along.

When I was a student like you, I learned how to read, write, and speak English in school because my parents were immigrants who spoke a foreign tongue. You, too, can master English or any other language if you try. Start now! Even a hobby like collecting new words will pay off in future years and will cost you nothing.

Follow the leadership and guidance of your teacher when you do these exercises with care and attention. If you want extra credit, tackle some of the special assignments. Above all, make up your mind to improve your skill in writing or saying whatever you want in a better way.

Good luck to you!

Cordially yours,
Joseph Bellafiore

WITH THIS BOOK YOU WILL LEARN

SIMPLE SENTENCES

Whenever you say something, you put words together to express an idea. Usually, you talk about someone doing something. Other times you tell how something happened.

The following are simple sentences. (**S**＝Subject, **V**＝Verb)

Tony plays the guitar. **S**　 **V**	**Definition**
He ran the mile. **S**　**V**	A *simple sentence* is a group of words having one subject and one verb.
The Yanks won the game. 　 **S**　　　**V**	

You will notice that each sentence has a subject and a verb.

The *subject* is the doer, and it answers the question *Who?*

Who plays the guitar?	*Answer:*	Tony
Who ran the mile?	*Answer:*	He
Who won the game?	*Answer:*	Yanks

The *verb* is the action word, and it answers the question *What did the subject do?*

What does *Tony* do?	*Answer:*	plays
What did *He* do?	*Answer:*	ran
What did the *Yanks* do?	*Answer:*	won

> **PLEASE!**
> Don't write in this book.
> Use separate sheets.

1

Write the subject and the verb in each sentence below.

1 My friend lost his dog.

4 Louis likes folk music.

2 The car stopped at the light.

5 A watch tells time.

3 Our plane landed safely.

Incomplete Sentences

Now let's take a look at some groups of words that are NOT sentences. Something is missing in each sample.

NO SUBJECT

INCOMPLETE: **Blew the whistle for the end of the game.**

To make this a simple sentence,
tell who blew the whistle.

COMPLETE: The *referee* blew the whistle for the end of the game.
                     S

NO VERB

INCOMPLETE: **The crowd up on their feet to watch the game.**

To make this a simple sentence,
tell what the crowd did.

COMPLETE: The crowd *stood* up on their feet to watch the game.
                             V

INCOMPLETE THOUGHT

INCOMPLETE: **While waiting for the bus.**

To make this a simple sentence,
tell what happened.

COMPLETE: *We played* while waiting for the bus.
             S   **V**

■ **Let's review what we have learned.**

A simple sentence is a group of words containing a subject and a verb. To make sense, the sentence must say something about a person or a thing.

Try this one / **CAN YOU SPOT A SIMPLE SENTENCE?**

Which group of words is a *simple sentence?* Write *a, b,* or *c* and give the subject and verb.

1 *a.* Made from sugar, syrup, and oranges.

   b. Your package arrived this morning.

   c. Danger! High voltage wire.

2 *a.* Honor and glory to our nation's heroes.

   b. Best wishes to Alice!

   c. At the meeting, he said "hello."

3 *a.* After visiting the doctor, he felt better.

   b. Which included a profit of 10%.

   c. No tipping allowed in this restaurant.

4 *a.* Just music and news on the radio.

   b. If you want mustard on the sandwich.

   c. Last year we won the championship.

5 *a.* Wearing a diving belt and snorkel.

   b. A family of four needs $9,500 a year.

   c. A long hot summer in the big cities.

6 *a.* Mother sat at the wheel.

b. Yesterday for our weekend shopping.

c. Driving the car to the supermarket.

7　*a.* Somebody backing out of his driveway.

b. Bang! right into our station wagon.

c. He checked his rear-view mirror.

8　*a.* By his error, we lost the game.

b. No more excuses for lateness.

c. Coming to school by bicycle or by bus.

9　*a.* Streets, houses, parks, all full of rubbish.

b. A clean city welcomes visitors.

c. To breathe fresh air for health's sake.

10　*a.* Peddlers selling articles from pushcarts.

b. Those who offer you gold watches cheap.

c. I bought a wood statue carved in Spain.

Try another / **COMPLETE THESE SIMPLE SENTENCES**

Write the missing *subject* or *verb* needed to complete the idea in each group of words below.

1　The chubby boy ＿?＿ some more ice cream.

2　Our ＿?＿ brought the day's mail.

3　The alarm clock ＿?＿ me up this morning.

4　A little rain ＿?＿ the road slippery.

The art of writing is a way of putting words together to help us understand each other.

5 My___?___ wrote a note for the milkman.

6 The jeweler ___?___ my broken wrist watch.

7 Some baby guppies ___?___ in our fish tank.

8 For breakfast, Tom ___?___ orange juice and milk.

9 During recess, the ___?___ played ball in the yard.

10 To stop the bleeding, the___?___put a band-aid on the cut.

Test your knowledge / **MAKE THE SENSE COMPLETE**

Write the word needed to fit the meaning in each sentence.

1 The Verrazano Bridge (**separates, connects, divides**) Brooklyn and Staten Island.

2 The hunt for buried treasure (**dug, located, failed**) to find even one cent.

3 Charlie Chaplin said, "Laughter (**is, hides, rejects**) the relief from pain."

4 Museums (**peddle, conceal, display**) collections of sculptures, paintings, crafts, etc.

5 Today's teenagers (**prefer, enjoy, ignore**) hard rock, soft rock, and classical.

Shoot for the basket

WRITE SIMPLE SENTENCES

Answer the following questions by writing simple sentences. Make sure that each group of words you use contains a *subject* and a *verb* and makes a *complete* statement.

1 What is your favorite sport?

2 How much allowance do you get?

3 Why do you like holidays?

4 Who is your best friend?

5 How old will you be on your next birthday?

6 What kind of job would you like when you grow up?

7 Which flavor of ice cream do you prefer?

8 Who is your best-liked TV comedian?

9 Where do they keep mystery stories in the school library?

10 Why must you exercise every day?

In This Lesson We Learned

A *simple sentence* contains one subject and one verb and expresses a complete thought.

SUBJECT MUST AGREE WITH VERB

LET'S REVIEW FIRST.

The **subject** of a sentence is the person or thing you are talking about. It answers the question *who?* or *what?*

John painted the model plane.
S

The *tree* broke during the storm.
S

The **verb** is the action word, telling what happened to the subject of the sentence or what the subject did.

Mary *caught* poison ivy on her heel.
V

The caterpillars *ate* the tomato leaves.
V

Now is the time to learn to use the basic tools of writing correctly and skillfully.

7

LET'S GO AHEAD!

The subject must agree with the verb in number.

A *singular subject* refers to one person or thing and requires a singular verb.

A true *patriot is* loyal to his country.
   s   **v**

This *road has* no sidewalk.
   s   **v**

A *plural subject* refers to two or more persons or things and requires a plural verb.

Some *men like* to play poker.
   s   **v**

Science *books teach* us about life.
   s   **v**

Quick quiz / **IS THE SUBJECT SINGULAR OR PLURAL?**

Can you choose the right *verb* to agree with the subject? Write it on your answer sheet.

1   Good talkers (*are* or *is*) also good listeners.

2   The fingers on your hand (*is* or *are*) clean and slim.

3   A bank for savings (*pay* or *pays*) interest on deposits.

4   A man lost in the woods (*does* or *do*) whatever needs doing.

5   If wishes (*was* or *were*) horses, then beggars would ride.

8

Compound Subject

AS A CONNECTIVE

Now let's take a look at a *compound subject*; that is, two subject words connected by *and*.

Lisa **and** *Matthew are* eating lunch together.
    s

The *cat* **and** the *canary are* watching each other.
    s

Above you see that two subject words require a plural verb: *are*.

OR

AS A CONNECTIVE

Suppose the two subject words are connected by *or*? Then the verb must agree with the word *nearer* to it.

John **or** his friends *are* to blame.

His friends **or** John *is* to blame.

After "either____or," "neither____nor," the verb agrees with the *nearer* subject.

Either those boys **or** this girl *was* whispering.

Neither she **nor** they *were* willing to admit it.

Quickie / **MAKE THE VERB AGREE WITH THE SUBJECT**

Can you figure out the correct choice of *verb*?

1   Honey and vinegar (*make, makes*) a special drink.

2   Coffee and buns *(is, are)* better than no breakfast.

3   Strangers or hikers *(wave, waves)* for a free ride.

4   A boy or his parents *(is, are)* to pay for damages.

5   Neither his parents nor the boy *(are, is)* willing to pay.

Subject After

*There is*_____   *There are*_____

*Here is*_____   *Here are*_____

These phrases used at the beginning of a sentence serve as an introduction for the subject which comes after. You must still make the verb agree with the subject, either singular or plural.

There **is** no *hope* left for the patient.   (SINGULAR)

s

There **are** many *reasons* for working.   (PLURAL)

s

Here **is** my *word* of honor.   (SINGULAR)

s

Here **are** *Ruth* and *Valerie*.   (PLURAL)

s

Follow the same rule when using these phrases in the past.

There **was** only *one* marked wrong.   (SINGULAR)

s

There **were** several *answers* acceptable.   (PLURAL)

s

Here **was** the *spot* where I found it.   (SINGULAR)

s

Here **were** the *stitches* in the hem.   (PLURAL)

s

$$\left.\begin{array}{l}\textit{There} \\ \textit{Here}\end{array}\right\} \textit{is/was} = \textbf{\textit{singular}}$$

$$\left.\begin{array}{l}\textit{There} \\ \textit{Here}\end{array}\right\} \textit{are/were} = \textbf{\textit{plural}}$$

Don't be tripped up! / **FIND THE REAL SUBJECT**

Can you find the *real subject* to match the verb?

1   There (are, is) my brother and sister.

2   Here (is, are) the kettle of fish.

3   There (is, are) someone who cares about you.

4   Here (are, is) your shoes and socks.

5   There (is, are) our friends and neighbors.

When Something Comes Between Subject and Verb

When a phrase or a clause stands between the subject and the verb, you must look carefully to find the true subject.

The *astronauts* | during their flight to the moon | *were* in contact
      s   **v**
with earth by radio.

The *men* | who directed their flight from the Space Center | *were*
   s   **v**
electronics experts.

11

In some everyday sentences, you may need to look twice before you decide whether the subject is the right one!

A box of cherries (is, are) expensive.

The Department of Parks (are, is) in charge.

The members of our team (are, is) experienced players.

Some neighbors on our block (is, are) a bit careless.

Do a little thinking to check your answers! One way of figuring these out is to leave the *phrase* out of the sentence.

A *box* | of cherries | *is* expensive.
  s   V

The *Department* | of Parks | *is* in charge.
      s   V

The *members* | of our team | *are* experienced players.
    s   V

Some *neighbors* | on our block | *are* a bit careless.
     s   V

Omit a PHRASE or CLAUSE to find the subject.

The same method can be used to clear away the *clause* that stands between a subject and a verb. Leave it out.

The girls who make the noise (is, are) rarely caught.

The *girls* _____ *are* rarely caught.
   s   V

The postman that delivers our letters (is, are) Angelo.

The *postman* _____ *is* Angelo.
    s   V

12

Choose wisely now! / **IGNORE THE PHRASE OR CLAUSE BETWEEN S + V**

Write the correct verb. Leave out what comes between the subject and the verb.

1 The chocolates in the tray (are, is) delicious.

2 That girl in red on skates (is, are) doing fancy tricks.

3 The fellow who sells hot dogs (are, is) very busy.

4 Some designers that set the style (is, are) young men.

5 Mountain springs instead of rivers (are, is) supplying drinking water.

Checkup test / **AGREEMENT OF SUBJECT WITH VERB**

Remember to have a singular subject followed by a singular verb; a compound subject takes a plural verb. Notice carefully how many persons or things take part in the action; one or more?

Write the verb that agrees with the subject in number.

1 There (*were* or *was*) a boy and a girl in the horse.

2   We (*were* or *was*) on our way home from the game.

3   I know there (*is* or *are*) lots of ways of earning money.

4   John and Lee (*is* or *are*) among my best friends.

5   Some pupils in the lunchroom (*are* or *is*) quite noisy.

6   The voters who elected him mayor (*says* or *say*) they made a mistake.

7   They (*was* or *were*) only talking in a whisper together.

8   A flock of birds in the sky (*was* or *were*) flying southward.

9   There (*were* or *was*) lead and tin mixed together in the alloy.

10 Since everybody (*was* or *were*) on time, we got started earlier.

In This Lesson We Learned

The subject must *agree* with the verb in a sentence.

- Singular subjects require singular verbs; plural subjects require plural verbs.

- Compound subjects (two or more subject words connected by *and*) require plural verbs.

- If the two subjects are connected by *or,* then the verb must agree with the subject *nearer* to it.

AVOID FRAGMENTS

A sentence must have a subject and a verb in order to set forth a complete idea. The parts must be connected together to make sense. Do these groups of words make sense?

1   On the bus I met someone. <u>A friend of mine.</u>
    fragment

2   <u>John, the doctor's only son.</u> He became an auto mechanic.
    fragment

3   Everybody will come to the picnic. <u>Especially on a school day.</u>
    fragment

Put the pieces together like this to make good sentences and avoid fragments.

One complete sentence:

1   On the bus I met someone, a friend of mine.

2   John, the doctor's only son, became an auto mechanic.

3   Everybody will come to the picnic, especially on a school day.

Another way of putting these ideas together to avoid fragments is like this.

Two complete sentences:

1   On the bus I met someone. She was a friend of mine.

2   John was the doctor's only son. He became an auto mechanic.

3   Everybody will come to the picnic. I think so, especially on a school day.

You will notice from the previous samples that:

Definition	A *fragment* is a piece of a sentence. It may be a phrase or group of words lacking complete sense.

How to Avoid Fragments

A Connect the fragment to the main idea in order to form a good sentence.

FRAGMENT: In the mail she found a gift. *Which came by surprise.*

SENTENCE: In the mail she found a gift which came by surprise.

B Make a complete sentence by adding the subject or verb.

FRAGMENT: He dusted the home plate. *His turn at bat now.*

SENTENCE: He dusted the home plate. It was his turn at bat now.

A FEW ALLOWABLE FRAGMENTS FOR SPECIAL USE!

The reader supplies the missing words to complete the meaning.

Sometimes you will notice a fragment on public display. Such a shortcut is not a blunder but an attention-getter! The following acceptable fragments are used deliberately and not carelessly:

No postage necessary if mailed in the U.S.

Center lane for passing only.

Parking reserved for customers while shopping.

First try / **CAN YOU SPOT THE CARELESS FRAGMENT?**

Some of the following are complete sentences, some are allowable fragments, and some are careless fragments. Re-write the careless fragments by making them into *complete* sentences.

1 Her fall was an accident. Which may never happen again.

2 Roadside picnic area 1,000 feet ahead.

3 Come out! Wherever you are.

4 Check coat at your own risk. Beware of thieves.

5 Early next morning. We'll be packed and ready.

6 In winter we dress warmly. In summer coolly.

7 Three out! All out! (Baseball umpire)

8 No stopping for repairs on bridge. Keep moving.

9 The cashier left for lunch. Just as I reached the checkout counter at the supermarket.

10 We used to play "twenty-one-you're-it" and "water polo" in the Hillside Swimming Pool. Lots of fun for all the kids.

Try again / **WHICH ARE THE FRAGMENTS?**

Read these carefully. Make sentences by re-writing the fragments into *complete* statements. Leave the others as they are.

1 Cooking, my favorite rainy day pastime.

2 While we were rowing across the lake. The boat overturned.

3 Keep off the grass. This means you.

4 We watched a late movie last night. On Channel 5.

5 In the last lap of the relay race. Tom dropped the stick.

6 Here we are, sir. At your service!

7 Father never drives on Sundays. Too much traffic.

> *Sentence structure shows how you think.*
> *Think straight and you will write correctly.*

8 There's no use crying. Better luck next time.

9 Flavor in sauce depends on spices. A little basil, not too much.

10 Running wild, he stumbled against the door. Gasping and dripping wet with sweat.

FOR EXTRA CREDIT

Check your own written work (in your notebook, letters, themes, book reports, shop notes, etc.). Circle all careless fragments and then write out the full sentence for each one.

Brain-teaser / **FRAGMENTS FROM THE NEWS**

The following fragments appeared as headlines in the news. Of course, you know these were written deliberately to catch attention and not as careless errors.

Can you make complete sentences by supplying the missing words?

EXAMPLE:

Fragment: Man suspect in robbery

Sentence: Police arrested a man as a suspect in the recent robbery of a supermarket.

1 Basketball camp slated for summer training

2 2 women robbed of pocketbooks

3 Cable cut, 125 without phones

4 $50,000 bail set in kidnap case

18

5   Jerseyans taking to camping in increasing numbers

6   Jazz guitarist heading tonight's program

7   Funds voted for water treatment plant

8   European tourists to take look at Daytop Village

9   Senators to act on arms pact

10   Astronauts training for joint trip with Soviets

Story / **BOZO THE CLOWN**

Re-write these paragraphs, making sentences wherever you find careless fragments.

Bozo the clown was in real life a tall, fat man. With a puffy face and long, reddish-blond hair. He wore gold-rimmed glasses. And a big gold ring on his finger. He was twenty-five or thirty when I met him. But he had a paunch that usually comes after forty. He wore loose, light trousers and a shirt open at the collar. The shirttails hanging.

He wasn't really sloppy. Just free and easy. Without the painted smile and the red nose, his face looked more sad than funny. His brown eyes looked straight into yours. Quite a sad sack, yet kind and lovable toward children. Bozo, a nice guy and not a circus or TV clown in person.

Master these! / **CHANGE FRAGMENTS INTO SENTENCES**

Some statements below are incomplete. Change the fragments into sentences by supplying the necessary words or changing the punctuation to connect parts with the main idea. Leave the complete sentences as they are.

1   Tom turned away from the visitor. Just stared out the window.

2   Drink a glass of milk at each meal for health's sake.

3   Calcium for strong teeth and bone structure.

4   Handball, tennis, and ping-pong are man-to-man sports.

5   No body contact in sports like swimming, weight-lifting, and archery.

6   Early in the morning. We packed our lunch for a picnic.

7   I sat in the car quietly. Just my dog and the radio.

8   There is money in cutting lawns. For generous neighbors.

9   Air-conditioned classrooms? Then we'll have year-round school!

10   Vacation time brings relief. Like resting after working.

In This Lesson We Learned

A *fragment* is an incomplete sentence. You can change a fragment into a sentence in three ways:
- by supplying the missing subject or verb;
- by changing the punctuation to link the pieces;
- by connecting the fragment to the main idea.

We use complete sentences to make our meaning clear.

20

COMPOUND SENTENCES

You know that a *simple* sentence has one subject and one verb. Suppose we put a pair of simple sentences together? Let's see what happens when we combine them.

2 SIMPLE SENTENCES:

He ate like a horse.

His bulky figure showed it.

COMBINED INTO 1 SENTENCE:

He ate like a horse, *and* his bulky figure showed it.

This is called a **compound sentence** because it has 2 main ideas connected by *and*. Two other connectives are *but* and *or*.

Take giant steps with and / or / but.

Let's try some other combinations.

2 SIMPLE SENTENCES:

The doctor recommended a weight-reducing diet.

The fat man refused to follow it.

COMBINED INTO 1 SENTENCE:

The doctor recommended a weight-reducing diet, *but* the fat man refused to follow it.

2 SIMPLE SENTENCES:

Mary played the piano for fun.

She relaxed with teenage magazines.

COMBINED INTO 1 SENTENCE:

Mary played the piano for fun, *or* she relaxed with teenage magazines.

Definition	A compound sentence has 2 main ideas connected by *and/or/but*. It combines 2 simple sentences into 1 strong sentence.

Kick-off time / **COMBINING SIMPLE SENTENCES**

Combine simple sentences into *compound* sentences by connecting the ideas using *and/or/but*.

1   He swam like a fish. He liked staying under water.

2   We stopped at a pizzeria. We ordered a tomato-and-cheese pie.

3   You may use water color for the sky. You may try oil paint.

4   We must practice singing together more often. We will make a hit at the concert.

5   This looks like the right spot. There is nobody else around.

6   Boys play baseball. Girls prefer volleyball.

7   She was invited to stay. She really wanted to go home.

8   When buying a used car, have a mechanic check it. You may be stuck with a "lemon."

9   Susan was a bridesmaid. Mary went as guest of the family.

10   Thank heaven for past favors. Remember the value of prayer.

Gain ten yards / **WRITING COMPOUND SENTENCES**

Complete the following statements by adding a main clause to make each statement a *compound* sentence.

1 We arrived at the picnic grounds early, and ...

2 ... , but he won the potato sack race.

3 You could have corn on the cob and hamburgers, or else ...

4 The boys and girls tossed raw eggs to each other in one contest, and ...

5 ... , but the judges disagreed on the length of the rope for the tug-o-war.

6 Balloon popping under the chin between couples was very funny, and ...

7 The record-player blared out some popular tunes, but ...

8 ... , and everybody got some kind of prize for trying the games and events.

9 The teachers in charge called the outing a success, but ...

10 Some parents suggested we hold a carnival next year, or ...

Make a touchdown / **KNOW YOUR S-F-C's!**

For each group of words, write:

      S for *simple* sentence   (complete thought)

      F for sentence *fragment*   (incomplete thought)

      C for *compound* sentence (two main thoughts)

Then tell why you think so.

1 The lucky numbers were seven and eleven.

2 When we all sang "Happy Birthday!"

3 We have met the enemy, and they are ours.

4 At midnight, the music stopped and so we went home.

5 The father of the girl who invited us to her party.

6 New stores have a magic-eye door-opener.

7 Forgive and forget, or we will not be friends any more.

8 A clock-timer turns on the lights at six o'clock.

9 Which may help to keep burglars away from our house.

10 Wear your safety belt, or you may be sorry.

Show some muscle / **TRAVEL ABROAD**

Re-write the following paragraphs. Use strong compound sentences by combining simple sentences using *and/or/but*.

Young Americans travel to Europe in great numbers. Airlines offer bargain prices for students and young adults. Tourists like the economy-class fares. Some charter flights for groups of five run as low as $180 for a round trip from New York to London.

Teenagers live in cheaper rooms and ride bicycles. They see the world as the natives who live there. They avoid swanky hotels and expensive restaurants. Sometimes they camp out in the public parks during hot summer nights. By day, they stroll through museums and gardens. They lie on the sunny beaches.

In countries like Spain and Italy, these young Americans are welcome. In England and France, our teenagers find a certain coolness. Anyway, at the present bargain rates, travel is the thing to do. Fly, Barbara. Happy trip!

CAUTIONS

Avoid "ramblers." These are longwinded, stretched-out, boring sentences stringing along with *and/ and then/ and so.*

We were pitching horseshoes for fun, *and then* some other fellows came along, *and* they wanted to play too, *and so* we made up teams with partners.

Put a comma before the word bridges *and/ or/ but.*

_____, and_____

_____, or _____

_____, but_____

In This Lesson We Learned

- A *compound* sentence combines two main clauses into a single sentence.
- A compound sentence connects the two main clauses by using *and/or/but.*
- Avoid using long rambling sentences loosely tied by *and/ and then/and so.*

COMPLEX SENTENCES

A simple statement having just a subject and verb makes sense. Yet the same idea may be enlarged by the use of phrases and clauses.

A sentence says something. A simple sentence has a subject and a verb to express an idea. Examples of a *simple* sentence:

> She ate a slice of melon.

> He delivered the newspapers.

These are called simple sentences because they contain one main clause to tell what happened.

Suppose you want to tell a little more; for example, *when? where? why? how?* You will have to add a helping clause. The following are called *complex* sentences because they have a *helping clause* to round out the *main clause.*

> She ate a slice of melon because she was hungry.
> _____   _____
>   main clause   helping clause

> He delivered the newspapers when school was over.
> _____ _____
>   main clause   helping clause

Helping clauses answer the questions *when? where? why? how? which one? what kind?* Helping clauses cannot stand alone as sentences because they are not complete statements. They must be tacked on to a main clause to make sense. Examples:

The man <u>who lives on our block</u> owns the grocery.
　　　　　helping clause

(who lives on our block→helping clause; *not* a sentence)

The tree <u>that stood near the fence</u> fell during the storm.
　　　　　helping clause

(that stood near the fence→helping clause; *not* a sentence)

Now you are ready to understand the definition:

> A *complex sentence* has a main clause and a helping clause to express an idea.

Write it right now / **YOU *CAN* WRITE COMPLEX SENTENCES**

Re-write these groups of words, supplying helping clauses in order to make the statements into *complex sentences.*

EXAMPLE:　He spoke to the bus driver because ...
　　　　　He spoke to the bus driver because *he wanted to get off*.

1　The Teen Club elected Mary president because ...

2　When ... they planned a skating party.

3　The man who ... is the owner of the garage.

4　You should have been stopped at the corner after ...

5　Some songs make you feel happy while ...

6   Here are the blue fish that . . .

7   The frame house where . . . still stands on the hill.

8   Why . . . is one of the puzzles of science.

9   How . . . if it starts raining?

10   Put your earnings in a savings account which . . .

Get a perfect score / **SIMPLE, COMPOUND, COMPLEX
SENTENCES**

Can you tell which are the *complex sentences* below? Remember this: a complex sentence has a main clause and a helping clause beginning with *when, who, that, if,* etc.

On your answer sheet, label each sentence by these abbreviations:

CX=complex sentence

CD=compound sentence

S=simple sentence

1   Please come over as soon as you are ready.

2   When it rains, wear your hat and rubbers.

3   If you make it yourself, you will save money.

4   The hills are full of trees, and the rivers are full of fish.

5   Take your time, Mary.

6   What is the reason that taxes keep growing every year?

7   An old saying runs like this: "You should go where the rain goes."

8   A balanced meal contains the basic food elements.

28

9   Some people are kind to strangers, but others shy away.

10   You should be loyal to your family who really care for you.

HOW CAN YOU MAKE USE OF COMPLEX SENTENCES?

To cut down a string of long rambling sentences (*and, and so, and then*), or else to tie together some simple sentences, you can break up the monotony by using complex sentences.

WEAK MONOTONY	BETTER VARIETY
He played the piano. He felt lonely, *and* the music gave him company, *and so* he banged out a rollicking tune, *and then* his mood carried him away. This was not an escape. It was a safe harbor to return to at will. Music is a companion. It can cheer you up.	*When* he felt lonely, he played the piano. The music gave him company *as* he banged out a rollicking tune. His mood carried him away. This was not an escape *but* a safe harbor to return to at will. Music is a companion *because* it can cheer you up.
(5 simple sentences and 1 long rambling sentence)	**(2 simple sentences with 3 complex sentences)**

Explanation:

By using the helping clauses beginning with *when, as, because* and by using *but* instead of the same old *and so, and then,* you can improve your writing. Be strong in saying what you want. Use some complex sentences whenever you can. (Like this last one.)

To show how a less important idea may be tied in with a more important idea, use a helping clause connected with a main clause.

A. WEAK:

(*2 simple sentences. No connection shown between ideas.*)

Mother gave mouth-to-mouth breath to help the baby. The emergency squad arrived with an oxygen tank.

STRONG:

(1 *complex sentence showing connection between ideas.*)

Mother gave mouth-to-mouth breath to help the baby *until* the emergency squad arrived with an oxygen tank.

B. WEAK:

(2 *simple sentences. No connection shown between ideas.*)

In case of accident, send for a doctor or a policeman. You may give first aid to an injured person.

STRONG:

(1 *complex sentence showing connection between ideas.*)

In case of accident, you may give first aid to an injured person *while* you send for a doctor or a policeman.

Explanation:

In the previous sentences (A and B), you find one idea is less important than the other. To show which one is less important, use a helping clause beginning with *until* or *while,* or some other connecting word. This way you tie the two simple sentences together into one strong complex sentence. Not just grammar, but power of thinking is developed. You can do it if you try! (Check this last sentence.)

Target for today / **COMBINING SIMPLE SENTENCES INTO COMPLEX SENTENCES**

Re-write the sentences that follow by combining 2 simple sentences into 1 complex sentence. Use the connecting words listed on the next page to show the thought relation between ideas.

EXAMPLE: 2 *simple* sentences:

He sold brushes for Fuller.
He made 40% on sales.

Combined into 1 *complex* sentence:

When he sold Fuller brushes, he made 40% on sales.

30

CONNECTING WORDS			
when	who	unless	while
where	that	until	before
why	how	as	after
because	since	if	although

1   We got up early. The sun came over the hill.

2   I will keep this for security. You must pay back the money.

3   They went back to the place. They used to go there during vacations.

4   You want to join the club. Do what I tell you.

5   Now you know the truth. I came just to be friends again.

6   Take care in handling this. It is highly inflammable stuff.

7   It was still raining hard. We decided to hike through the green belt along the highway.

8   The Indian was over a hundred years old. He told us the true story of General Custer's last stand.

9   My tooth broke. The dentist was filling a cavity.

10   I felt no pain. The novocain deadened my nerves.

Right on! / **ARE YOU A JOINER?**

Re-write these paragraphs using *complex* sentences for variety. You may combine two simple sentences, or you may break up long rambling compound sentences.

Youngsters need to belong to groups. They like to join clubs. They make teams. They form bands. They help in church and community affairs. In this way they feel they are doing something

31

worthwhile, and they like to be part of the "action," and they proudly show off their badges or uniforms.

Young boys and girls are trying to find themselves as persons. They want to know their abilities and their weaknesses, and they want to compare themselves with others, yet they are not exactly sure of what they are looking for.

Thank God that sports and clubs provide a good way of getting youngsters together. These are an outlet for energy. They offer a chance for leadership. They avoid the boredom of doing nothing. How about you?

FOR EXTRA CREDIT

Copy neatly or clip carefully from a newspaper or old magazine three samples of each kind of sentence studied so far:

(a) **simple** → **1** main clause

(b) **compound** → **2** main clauses

(c) **complex** → **1** main clause **+1** helping clause

You should be able to handle each type in your own speaking and writing to give greater clearness and force to whatever you wish to say.

In This Lesson We Learned

A *complex sentence* has a main clause and a helping clause.

• It combines two simple sentences into one complex sentence for better thought-relationship.

• It breaks up long rambling compound sentences for variety.

NOUNS

WHAT'S IN A NAME?

A name is our way of calling somebody or something in order to be able to tell these persons or things apart from others. It is much better than saying, "Hey, you!" or "Whozis?" or "Whatzit?"

What Is a Noun?

> A *noun* is a word used to name anybody, any place, any thing. It answers these questions: *Who? Where? What?*
>
> 1 A word that names a *person* is a noun:
>
> > friend, doctor, Patrick, Florence, dancer, brother, painter, driver, stranger, visitor
>
> 2 A word that names a *place* is a noun:
>
> > city, country, school, house, garden, bank, library, store, Rome, Tokyo
>
> 3 A word that names a *thing* is a noun:
>
> > pencil, chair, boat, television, radio, sandwich, typewriter, ring, United Nations, peace

Write nouns that name persons, places, things. Arrange your answer sheet in three columns as below.

PERSONS	PLACES	THINGS
1 __?__	6 __?__	11 __?__
2 __?__	7 __?__	12 __?__
3 __?__	8 __?__	13 __?__
4 __?__	9 __?__	14 __?__
5 __?__	10 __?__	15 __?__

Why Are Some Nouns Spelled With Capital Letters?

You must have noticed already that some nouns begin with a capital letter while other nouns start with a small letter. Why?

For example, when you are writing about the many rivers that flow around the earth, you just write *rivers* with a small letter. But when you pick out a special river or name a single particular river, you write the noun with capital letters:

Hudson River
Potomac River

The capital letter shows that the noun refers to a special person, place, or thing. It may be a single member of a group.

Notice the difference between these two spellings:

1 All <u>rivers</u> run into the sea.
   small letter

2 The **C**onnecticut **R**iver is polluted by industrial wastes.
   capital letters

Common or Proper Nouns?

These two kinds of nouns are simply an easy way to remember the right spelling:

common nouns → **small letters**
     I met two guys shopping.

proper nouns → **capital letters**
     I went to **T**wo **G**uys **S**hopping **C**enter.

Ready? Go! / **ARE THEY COMMON OR PROPER NOUNS?**

 On your answer paper, write the proper nouns with capital letters, but leave the common nouns as they are.

boys	pools	the white house
girls	olympics	a white house
greece	bicycles	a bell
france	columbia	the liberty bell
roads	england	a giant
buick	george	the giants team
cars	albany	a rocket
cadillac	lawyers	the rockettes

Capitalize a particular person or place or thing.

35

Show respect, please! / **CAPITALIZE PROPER NOUNS**

Write the proper nouns which have been printed in small letters but should be capitalized.

Capitalize nouns which are particular or special, such as individual persons, named areas, labeled things.

1 Modern rome has preserved the ruins of the old coliseum.

2 In the harbor stands the statue of liberty to welcome you.

3 From the eiffel tower you can see almost all of paris.

4 Sunset in mallorca makes the cathedral in palma look like gold.

5 The rotary club of staten island meets at the tavern-on-the-green.

6 Have you seen the niagara falls from the canadian side?

7 Bob served as a member of the federal grand jury once.

8 The united nations seeks to establish peace around the world.

9 Where does the missouri river meet the mississippi river?

10 The wandering moors sailed to sicily and granada.

11 The liberal party threw its votes to the democratic party.

12 Captain james cook was an english navigator and explorer.

13 For the latest news about stocks, read the wall street journal.

14 Someday travel to beautiful waikiki beach in honolulu.

15 You will find your civil liberties listed in the bill of rights.

FOR EXTRA CREDIT

Keep a list in your notebook of five or more proper nouns that you notice in such places as the following:

street signs	neighborhood churches
department stores	newspaper articles
community agencies	pantry shelf items

Warm-up time / **NAME THE PERSON, PLACE, THING**

Complete these sentences with nouns.

HINT: The number in parentheses tells you the number of missing letters you need to spell the nouns.

1 Who was our first President?

(10) was our first President.

2 What is the short word for automobile?

(3) means automobile.

3 Which is the capital of France?

(5) is the capital of France.

4 What is the title of the person who is the head of a school?

The (9) is the head of a school.

5 TV is the abbreviation for what object of communication?

TV is the abbreviation for (10).

These are easy / **COMMON NOUNS**

Write the ordinary common nouns that fit these situations.

1 The __?__ lost her dog.

2 __?__ is the opposite of night.

3   During the summer, we sometimes go to the __?__.

4   When we feel thirsty, we drink some __?__.

5   Where there is smoke, there is __?__.

How Are Nouns Used in Sentences?

In the following sentences, the nouns are underlined.

Nouns are used either as the subject **(S)** or the object **(O)** while naming a person, place, or thing in the sentence.

1   <u>Columbus</u> discovered <u>America</u>.
     (S) person   **(O) place**

2   <u>Milk</u> is usually served in a <u>glass</u>.
     (S) thing   **(O) thing**

3   <u>Harry</u> lost his <u>watch</u> in <u>school</u>.
     (S) person   **(O) thing** **(O) place**

4   Former <u>President Eisenhower</u> wrote his own <u>story</u> of the <u>war</u>.
                  (S) person   **(O) thing**   **(O) thing**

5   <u>Father</u> watched the <u>game</u> on <u>television</u> at <u>home</u> yesterday.
     (S) person   **(O) thing** **(O) thing**   **(O) place**

We challenge you / **SPOT THE NOUNS**

Write the nouns in these sentences and label each noun as a person, place, or thing.

For extra credit, write *S* for subject and *O* for object.

1   Canada has a cold climate.

2   Gold was discovered in California during the Gold Rush.

38

3   Louise and her brother play golf fairly well.

4   George Washington is called "The Father of our country."

5   Henry Ford made the first automobile.

Keep improving your writing / **USING NOUNS**

Write sentences using these groups of words containing nouns.

1   the *captain* of the *team*

2   an unexpected *rain*

3   an exciting *game*

4   the tired *players*

5   in the *kitchen*

6   under the *porch*

7   the *sound* of *music*

8   our marching *band*

9   the cheering *crowd*

10   my last *quarter*

In This Lesson We Learned

A *noun* is a name-word for a person, place, or thing.

- Capitalize proper nouns referring to a particular member of a group.
- Use small letters for common nouns referring to a general group.
- A noun is used as either subject or object in a sentence.

PLURALS OF NOUNS

Note well!

When a noun refers to one thing, the noun is *singular*.

a street	an eagle
the house	any day
one apple	the animal
a dish	the beach

When a noun refers to more than one thing, the noun is *plural*.

SINGULAR +<u>S</u> = PLURAL		SINGULAR +<u>ES</u> = PLURAL	
street	streets	dish	dishes
house	houses	peach	peaches
apple	apples	watch	watches
diamond	diamonds	pass	passes

You will notice that the nouns above *form the plural* by just **adding s or es to the singular noun.** Learn this rule now and you will be right about 99 times out of 100 in spelling plural nouns.

Quick quiz / **WRITE PLURALS OF NOUNS**

Try this little quiz. Write the *plurals*.

SINGULAR NOUNS		PLURAL NOUNS
1 a door	→	some d __?__
2 one orange	→	two o __?__
3 the shoe	→	the s __?__
4 that person	→	those p __?__
5 our church	→	our c __?__
6 the brush	→	the b __?__
7 this desk	→	these d __?__
8 any year	→	several y __?__
9 your box	→	your b __?__
10 an elephant	→	all e __?__

Good English is easier when you follow the rules of language.

KEY   Add *s* to all except *es* for 5, 6 and 9 (which end in *ch*, *sh*, and *x*).

Now, let's take a look at the nouns that do not follow the rule. There really are not many of these "irregular" nouns, but you might as well know them and get 100% whenever you meet them. Watch the spelling!

41

Rule	Nouns ending in a *consonant* **+** *y* change the *y* to *i* and add *es*.

pony—ponies   cooky—cookies

sky—skies   dummy—dummies

party—parties   liberty—liberties

baby—babies   democracy—democracies

candy—candies   memory—memories

Please notice that the above nouns all end in a *consonant* with a *y*, and require a change in spelling from *y* to *i*.

Rule	When a noun ends in a *vowel* (a, e, i, o, u) with a *y*, it follows the regular rule of just adding an *s*.

way—ways   buy—buys

toy—toys   joy—joys

key—keys   donkey—donkeys

turkey—turkeys   monkey—monkeys

Rule	Nouns ending in *f* change the *f* to *v* and add *es*; nouns ending in *fe* change *fe* to *ve* and add *s*.

leaf—leaves   knife—knives

loaf—loaves   life—lives

calf—calves   wife—wives

shelf—shelves   penknife—penknives

There are a few exceptions to this rule. A few nouns ending in *f* or *fe*, make no change in spelling; just add an *s*.

chief—chiefs   cafe—cafes

roof—roofs   giraffe—giraffes

Rule	Most nouns ending in *o* add an *s* for the plural.

piano—pianos   cameo—cameos

solo—solos   alto—altos

memo—memos   soprano—sopranos

A few common exceptions to this rule include these nouns ending in *o* that add an *es* to form the plural.

hero—heroes   domino—dominoes

tomato—tomatoes   potato—potatoes

hobo—hoboes   no—noes (opposite of *yeses*)

Odd plurals include these words:

child—children   tooth—teeth

man—men   mouse—mice

woman—women   foot—feet

RULES FOR FORMING PLURALS OF NOUNS

I   Most nouns simply add *s*.
Nouns ending in a hissing sound (s, sh, ch, x, z) add *es*.

II Nouns ending in consonant + *y*, change *y* to *i* and add *es*.
Nouns ending in vowel + *y*, just add *s*.

III Nouns ending in *f*, change *f* to *v* and add *es*.
Nouns ending in *fe*, change *fe* to *ve* and add *s*.

IV Nouns ending in *o*, add *s*.

Practice makes perfect / **MORE PLURALS OF NOUNS**

A Write the *plural* for these regular nouns. (**Rule I**)

1 paper   *3* light   *5* idea   *7* flower

2 flag   *4* cent   *6* game   *8* clock

43

9 driver	12 pencil	15 captain	18 village
10 statue	13 dinner	16 friend	19 quarter
11 summer	14 noise	17 scene	20 propeller

B Write the *plural* for these nouns. (**Rule I**)

1 match	6 buzz	11 dash	16 rosebush
2 witch	7 tax	12 waltz	17 rash
3 dish	8 bus	13 box	18 march
4 wish	9 lunch	14 fox	19 couch
5 guess	10 fish	15 wristwatch	20 business

C Some of these nouns change *y* to *i* and add *es* to form the plural. Others just add *s*. (**Rule II**)

1 journey	6 study	11 city	16 candy
2 quantity	7 secretary	12 buoy	17 bay
3 laboratory	8 X-ray	13 nursery	18 survey
4 delay	9 turkey	14 relay	19 duty
5 convoy	10 opportunity	15 buddy	20 ability

DEATH OF A HERO

For each underscored noun, write its *plural* on your answer sheet. (**Rules I, II, III, IV**)

It was a quiet <u>evening</u> on the <u>farm</u>. The <u>owner</u> and his <u>friend</u>

were having some coffee with the busy <u>wife</u>. On the <u>radio</u>, a local soprano was singing a sweet lullaby while accompanied by a piano and a guitar. Outside in the tomato patch, a stray fox crept along. He was a chicken thief hungry for a meal. He did not rustle a leaf as he approached the hen house. The farmer kept a gun and a knife on the door just in case of need. A field mouse ran across the porch. The sound stirred the listeners inside. As they got up, the fox stepped on a home-made trap which slammed a box over him. It was not the death of a hero!

MEET THE CHALLENGE

This mastery test includes all the rules. Re-write these sentences making each italicized noun plural and certain other changes to make the sentence correct.

EXAMPLE: He paid the *man* a *dollar.*

He paid the *men* two *dollars.*

45

1   As a result of the *accident,* Tommy lost a front *tooth.*

2   Donna borrowed her mother's powder *puff* before the *party.*

3   A good *secretary* answers the office *buzz* promptly.

4   This *sandwich* tastes better with sliced *pickle.*

5   When the *soprano* hit high C, they tossed a *tomato.*

6   Men had to defend their *belief* in *democracy.*

7   On a national *holiday,* we hang out the *flag.*

8   A giant *searchlight* helps the *pilot* spot the airport.

9   Put the garage *key* back on the *hook* next time.

10   Once in his *life* he sharpened the kitchen *knife.*

In This Lesson We Learned
- Most nouns form their *plural* by adding *s* or *es.*
- Nouns ending in *y, f, fe,* and *o* follow special rules.
- A few odd plurals must be memorized.

POSSESSIVE NOUNS

Grammar is not just a classroom exercise; it is a valuable tool for putting forth your ideas the right way.

To show that a thing belongs to people, we use an easy spelling signal: an apostrophe and an *s*. For example:

Whose hat is this?   It belongs to Tom.   It is **Tom's** hat.
Whose coat is this?   It belongs to Mary.   It is **Mary's** coat.

You will notice that the nouns show ownership or "belonging to" by means of a spelling signal: an apostrophe and an *s*: Tom**'s**, Mary**'s**. These nouns are called *possessive nouns* **because they show ownership or "belonging to."**

How Do You Write the Possessive of Singular Nouns?

In order to show ownership, **you write the possessive of a singular noun by adding an apostrophe and an *s*.** The possessive noun tells you to whom the thing belongs. For example:

the license belongs to the **driver**   →   the **driver's** license
the hat belongs to the **man**   →   the **man's** hat
the trunk of the **elephant**   →   the **elephant's** trunk
the nest of the **bird**   →   the **bird's** nest
the dress of the **lady**   →   the **lady's** dress

Can you write the *possessive nouns* for these?

1 the wife of the **farmer**   →   the __?__ wife

2 the book belongs to the **girl**   →   the __?__ book

3 the post of the **enemy**   →   the __?__ post

4 the recipe of my **mother**   →   my __?__ recipe

5 the mustache of my **father**   →   my __?__ mustache

All the nouns mentioned so far are *singular nouns,* referring to only one person or thing. All of them formed the possessive the same way; you just had to add an apostrophe and an *s.* Easy to remember! Only one exception is allowed: a singular noun ending in *s* requires just an apostrophe.

Lewis=Lewis'/Dickens=Dickens'/Jones=Jones'

How to Write the Possessive of Plural Nouns

Now, let's take a look at *plural nouns.* Here we find a bit of a problem because some plurals end in *s* and some do not end in *s.* **The nouns that *end in s* need just an apostrophe at the end:** friends' / neighbors' / citizens' / laborers' / workers' / students' / fathers' / mothers' / etc.

the committee of **friends**   →   the **friends'** committee

the lawn of our **neighbors**   →   our **neighbors'** lawn

the spokesman for the **citizens** →   the **citizens'** spokesman

the organizer for the **workers** →   the **workers'** organizer

But whenever the plural noun does *not end in s,* **you have to add an apostrophe and an** *s* **to form the possessive.** Watch the endings!

the lunch for the **children**	→ the **children's** lunch
the club for the **women**	→ the **women's** club
the lounge for the **men**	→ the **men's** lounge
the trail of the **deer**	→ the **deer's** trail

A HANDY BOX SCORE OF POSSESSIVE NOUNS

ALL SINGULAR NOUNS	**ADD 'S** boy + 's → a boy's watch girl + 's → a girl's bracelet country + 's → our country's flag *Exception:* Dickens + ' → Dickens' novels
PLURAL NOUNS *NOT* **ENDING IN** *S*	**ADD 'S** men + 's → the men's locker people + 's → the people's choice children + 's → the children's pool
PLURAL NOUNS ENDING IN *S*	**ADD '** scouts + ' → scouts' code travelers + ' → travelers' luggage ladies + ' → ladies' lounge

★ Another easy way of fixing these rules in your memory is to look at the noun ending first.

If it does *not* end in s, you add an apostrophe and s. If it ends in s, you add only an apostrophe.

Try another / **WRITING POSSESSIVE NOUNS**

Write the *possessive noun* for each of the following.

1	the car belonging to my **brother**	my __?__ car
2	the óffice of the **doctor**	the __?__ office
3	the motto of our **school**	our __?__ motto
4	the uniform for the **team**	our __?__ uniform
5	the leader of our **country**	our __?__ leader
6	the hairdresser for the **ladies**	the __?__ hairdresser
7	the trophy for our **cheerleaders**	our __?__ trophy
8	the bicycles for some **boys**	some __?__ bicycles
9	the bench for the **players**	the __?__ bench
10	the workroom for our **teachers**	our __?__ workroom

Shoot for the basket / **POSSESSIVE NOUNS**

Write the *correct possessive* form for the italicized noun.

1 The courtroom waited eagerly for the *jury* verdict in the case.

2 The Army granted permission for the *soldiers* brides to return home with the men.

3 When Matthew became of age, he joined the *engineers* union.

4 My *brother* condition after the accident started to improve.

5 The *youngsters* appetites called for more food and drink.

6 The hot branding iron burned the ranch mark on the *cattle* hides.

7 Krista Carlson forgot her new comb in the *girls* washroom.

8 After election, some *politicians* promises are quickly forgotten.

50

9   We expected our *principal* visit to our class on Monday.

10 The traffic *officer* whistle directed
the cars at the crossing.

Score 100% / **POSSESSIVE NOUNS**

Write the *possessive form* for each noun below.

SINGULAR NOUNS				PLURAL NOUNS			
1	door	6	sister	11	visitors	16	oceans
2	person	7	author	12	salesmen	17	rings
3	class	8	rabbit	13	puppies	18	women
4	father	9	eagle	14	voters	19	marines
5	pal	10	friend	15	candidates	20	kittens

In This Lesson We Learned

Possessive nouns show ownership by an *apostrophe* or by an *apostrophe s*, depending on the ending.

WORD-STUDY USING NOUNS

Whatever you can rightly label with a word becomes the personal property of your mind.

One of the ways of building up your knowledge of words and their meanings is to study nouns that are the *same* and to learn their *opposites*. For example, are the following pairs the same or opposite?

    A   game / contest

    B   rocks / stones

    C   hunger / satisfaction

Answers: *A* = same; *B* = same; *C* = opposite.

52

EXERCISES

A Write the words that fit the statements. To help you spot the words, the first and last letters are given. As a clue, the number of missing letters is indicated in parentheses.

1 A thing that regulates the flow of water is a **F (4) T.**

2 A person who pays wages to others to work for him is an **E (6) R.**

3 A place where trains stop to let people on or off is a **S (5) N.**

4 Some statues are chiseled out of a kind of stone called **M (4) E.**

5 Meat and fish cooked over an open charcoal **F (2) E** are broiled.

6 The fellow who calls the balls and strikes in baseball is an **U (4) E.**

7 In Holland the sea is kept out of the land by means of **D (3) S.**

8 Watch repairs should be made by a **J (5) R.**

9 The prize for the winning team will be a beautiful **T (4) Y.**

10 When sounds by instruments harmonize, you hear good **M (3) C.**

B Can you tell which pairs of nouns are the same *or* opposite in meaning? Write *S* for the same; write *O* for the opposite.

1	laughter	/	tears	*6*	pursuit	/	retreat
2	life	/	death	*7*	regret	/	sorrow
3	find	/	discovery	*8*	friend	/	enemy
4	crackers	/	cookies	*9*	victory	/	defeat
5	wages	/	salary	*10*	youngster	/	oldtimer

C   Write the *noun* that fits the meaning in each sentence.

1   The fastest running animal of those in parentheses is the (**squirrel, elephant, horse**).

2   A person who damages property may be called a (**hero, vandal, loafer**).

3   Sudden changes in the weather may have a bad effect on a farmer's (**barn, roadway, crops**).

4   Walking instead of riding to go places is recommended for losing excess (**muscle, weight, bone**).

5   Your career or job is called your (**hobby, pastime, vocation**).

6   A short "break" during a performance is listed on the program as (**intermission, welcome, farewell**).

7   Sometimes you will find a natural spring at the top of a (**valley, dale, mountain**).

8   A newcomer on any job is usually called a (**veteran, oldtimer, recruit**).

9   One of our basic human needs is (**success, pain, failure**).

10   Our baker won a prize for a wedding cake because of its unusual (**layers, decorations, price**).

D   Write the *opposite* word.

1	war	6	right
2	silence	7	questions
3	adult	8	distance
4	ignorance	9	warmth
5	strength	10	amateur

E Write a word with the *same* meaning.

11 permission

12 result

13 effort

14 calmness

15 workroom

16 courage

17 burden

18 cafeteria

19 perfume

20 plaything

ACTION VERBS

Action verbs show what is happening. They tell you what someone or something is doing or has done.

Eva *ate* a chocolate cookie. (*ate* is an action verb)
Tony *fell* into the water. (*fell* shows what happened)

Lightning *struck* the tree. (*struck* shows action)
The plane *landed* safely. (*landed* tells what happened)

There are thousands of action verbs. Here are a few samples:

walk	spend	help	start
talk	save	love	stop
eat	read	hate	go
sleep	write	win	catch
play	sing	hop	drop
work	dance	skip	hold
study	lose	jump	cut

Quickie / **ACTION VERBS**

Now put verbs into *action* by combining them with subject words. Use the tense of the verb that fits the time of the action or happening.

1 walk   We __?__ to the theater last night.

56

2	*save*	You __?__ when you shop in a supermarket.
3	*love*	A child __?__ his own parents best of all.
4	*help*	Neighbors __?__ other people in trouble.
5	*sleep*	If you __?__ all day, you waste time.

WHERE IS THE ACTION?

Action verbs tell about two kinds of action: body and mind.

An action of the *body* would include your "doings"	An action of the *mind* would refer to your "doings"
PHYSICALLY	MENTALLY
I ate	I thought
I slept	I planned
I played	I hoped
I worked	I wondered
etc.	etc.

When did it happen? / **TELL THE TIME OF THE ACTION**

Complete these sentences with the action verbs in parentheses. Use the tense of the verb that fits the time of the action or happening.

1   Sometimes I *(wish)* that I were a bit older and got more of an allowance every week.

2   The firemen held the safety net ready while the man on the roof *(jump)* for his life.

3   If you *(swim)* before breakfast, you may get a sharper appetite for bacon and eggs.

4   My brother-in-law has a sticker on his car bumper saying, "I'd rather be *(fly)*!"

5   Boys and girls *(dance)* together in some of the amusing scenes of the comedy.

6   We always *(dream)* of the day to come when there will be peace among all people of the world.

7   Will you please *(write)* me a postcard telling me about your trip to the country?

8   A good housekeeper *(clean)* on a regular schedule, whereas a poor one lets everything go.

9   Most parents *(hope)* that their children will turn out successful in life.

10   The bank guard *(surprise)* the masked bandit by tackling him as he ran toward the door.

Get things moving along /   **USING ACTION VERBS**

Write ten sentences using the action verbs listed below.

1	build	6	guess
2	sell	7	call
3	buy	8	lose
4	slice	9	pray
5	plan	10	draw

Same or opposite? / WORD-STUDY BASED ON ACTION VERBS

Are these pairs of verbs **S** *(same)* or **O** *(opposite)* in meaning?

1	accept	/ reject
2	connect	/ separate
3	conceal	/ reveal
4	bother	/ annoy
5	gather	/ collect
6	fight	/ struggle
7	threaten	/ menace
8	destroy	/ preserve
9	wake	/ drowse
10	shelter	/ protect

In This Lesson We Learned

Action verbs show what the subject does or did. The action may be a mental or physical happening.

LINKING VERBS

Linking verbs connect the subject of the sentence with another word that tells us something about the subject.

The most common linking verbs are these:

be (am, are, is, was, were)			
appear	seem	grow	} verbs of **being**
look	become	remain	

look	smell	feel	} verbs of the **5 senses**
taste	sound		

As you read these sentences, notice how the linking verbs connect the subject with another word. The "other word" tells something about the subject: *who? what? how?*

The class president is <u>Mary Ann.</u>
    S   V   Who?

Tom became a skillful <u>painter.</u>
  S   V   What?

The air-conditioning felt <u>good.</u>
    S   V How?

Linking verbs are different from *action verbs*. The linking verbs serve as a connection between the subject and a noun or an adjective used to say something about the subject. The linking verb could be set down as an equal sign like this:

Louis is tall.   (Louis=tall.)

An action verb tells what the subject *does;* a linking verb names or describes the subject. Another way of telling these two kinds of verbs apart is to remember this box.

action verb—verb of **doing**

linking verb—verb of **being,** or **5 senses**

LOOK   TASTE   SMELL   SOUND   FEEL

Verbs of the Five Senses

Can you tell them apart? / **VERBS: ACTION OR LINKING**

Select the verb in each sentence and write *action (A)* or *linking (L),* according to the way it is used.

1   My father planted six tomato seedlings in the back yard.

2   Uncle Louis became an artist with a check printing company.

3   During the summer, we enjoyed band concerts in the park.

4   The spare tire was bald and deflated.

5   Dad was happy to find the easy kind of jack-lift.

6   The right front wheel seemed flat, bumping along.

7   We were all experts in offering advice on how to do it.

8   A garage mechanic sold us two new tires for safety's sake.

9   Mother felt peeved over the cost, about seventy-five dollars.

10 Yes, I am ready, willing, and able to work now.

How would you say it? / **COMPLETION TEST USING LINKING VERBS**

   Write the *linking verb* that fits the meaning in each of the sentences below. Choose verbs of *being* or the *senses* listed on page 60.

1   Those dark clouds__?__threatening.

2   José and Anita__?__delighted with their wedding gifts.

3   Fresh strawberries and cream__?__delicious.

4   A velvet skirt__?__soft and rich.

5   I hope you will__?__tall and strong.

6   Cooking outdoors usually__?__a bit smoky.

7   Little blisters on the skin__?__irritating.

8   The field___?___muddy after the rain.

9   Thank God you do not___?___a youngster forever.

10   The old car___?___good after a washing and waxing.

HELPING VERBS

REVIEW

The main verb in a sentence shows action or state of being. You recognize the main verb by the fact that it carries the message by telling something about what the subject does or appears to be. It answers the question, "What's happening?"

The boy <u>delivered</u> the newspaper to our house.
      action

He <u>felt</u> tired at the end of his route.
linking

NEW IDEA

As you read the following sentences, you will notice that there are other words used to help the main verb say something. (**H.V.** = helping verb; **M.V.** = main verb.)

She <u>has</u> <u>learned</u> how to knit a pair of socks.
  H.V. **M.V.**

He <u>was</u> <u>skating</u> on thin ice near the edge.
  H.V.   **M.V.**

They <u>do</u> <u>make</u> smaller cars in foreign countries.
   H.V. **M.V.**

The main verbs are *learned, skating, make*. The other words used to help the main verbs are *has, was, do*.

64

> *Helping verbs* are used to form the tense (or time) and to emphasize the action of the verb.

Here are a few other examples of helping verbs used to strengthen the main verbs. The helpers come first; the main verb is the last word in the verb phrase.

I *could have* stayed at the pool all day.
          main

She *must have* put her bracelet on the dresser.
          main

We *should be* finished within forty minutes.
          main

> **The chief helping verbs are:** *be, have, do, can, may, will, shall.* The tenses of these verbs are listed below.
>
> | BE | HAVE | DO | CAN | MAY | WILL | SHALL |
> |----|------|-----|-------|-------|-------|--------|
> | am | has | does | could | might | would | should |
> | is | had | did | | must | | |
> | are | | | | | | |
> | was | | | | | | |
> | were | | | | | | |

Tie things together / **COMPLETING SENTENCES WITH HELPING VERBS**

Write the *helping verbs* needed to complete these sentences.

1 If I had known you were coming, I __?__ __?__ baked a cake.

2 When you do not feel well, you __?__ not want to have strangers.

3 Since it was raining, you __?__ __?__ worn your rubbers!

4   After putting the clothes in the dryer, you __?__ __?__ closed the door.

5   Such information __?__ __?__ found in the telephone directory.

6   He __?__ __?__ __?__ elected because of his record and experience.

7   That racehorse __?__ __?__ run much faster on a dry track.

8   Unfortunately, her diamonds __?__ stolen while she slept.

9   Putting them in a safe deposit box __?__ __?__ protected her jewels.

10 Now that the sun is out, we __?__ get a little tan outdoors.

FOR EXTRA CREDIT

Write or copy from newspapers or magazines ten sentences using some of these *helping verbs:*

be, have, do, can, may, will, shall

or any others listed in this lesson as helpers.

Help your writing / **HELPING VERBS IN SENTENCES**

Using the correct form of the helping verbs in the sentences that follow, answer the questions in complete sentences.

> **Q.** Will you please answer the phone?
> **A.** I will answer the phone.

1 Are you expecting a check in the mail?

2 Would you have come without an invitation to the party?

3 Must we obey all these rules all the time?

4 Have you learned how to swim in deep water?

5 May I have another cookie for a snack?

6 Were they cheering for the bull or the toreador?

7 Has the boy delivered the Sunday newspaper yet?

8 Do all workers receive their pay on Friday?

9 Couldn't they re-cycle empty beer cans in every town?

10 Does she have to chatter with her friend during the movie?

In This Lesson We Learned

Helping verbs are small words (*be, have, do, can, may, will, shall*, etc.) used to help the main verb. The helpers come first; the main verb is last in the verb phrase.

TENSE OF VERBS

You tell time by looking at a clock. The hands on the dial point to the hours and minutes. Right?

How can you tell the time of the action in a sentence? By looking for these three clues:

(1) Changes in spelling the main verb

PRESENT TENSE: We *ride* our bikes to school.
PAST TENSE: We *rode* our bikes to school.

PRESENT:	speak	find	drop	catch
PAST:	spoke	found	dropped	caught

(2) The use of helping verbs before the main verb

PRESENT TENSE: I *do* go out after school.
PAST TENSE: I *did* not go out the other day.
FUTURE TENSE: I *will* go out some time soon.

PRESENT:	I *am* going home.	We *are* having fun.
PAST:	I *was* going home.	We *were* having fun.
FUTURE:	I *will be* going home.	We *will be* having fun.

(3) Adverbs of time used to modify the verb

PRESENT:	now	today	before
	↓	↓	↓
PAST:	then	yesterday	after
	↓	↓	↓
FUTURE:	next	tomorrow	soon

68

SUMMARY

To tell the time of the action in a sentence, look for these 3 clues: changes in spelling, helping verbs, adverbs of time.

HELPFUL HINTS FOR TENSE

You can guess the time by the words used to answer the question.

WHEN?

PRESENT	PAST	FUTURE
now	then	next
today	yesterday	tomorrow
do	did	will
are	were	shall
is	was	will be

Clock work / **CAN YOU EXPRESS THE RIGHT TIME OF THE ACTION?**

Write short sentences answering these questions. Use the right time (or tense) to fit the action.

1 When do we eat? (*Present*)

2 When did you ride the bus? (*Past*)

3 When will you learn to skate? (*Future*)

4 When do you expect to graduate? (*Present*)

5 When did you read that story? (*Past*)

6   When will you call your brother? *(Future)*

Once upon a time / **THE TIME IS <u>PAST</u>**

Write the *past* tense of each italicized verb.

1   Bob *is* playing golf.

2   Anne *has* her son vacuuming the rugs.

3   Dorothy *likes* hamburgers cooked medium rare.

4   Eric *handles* the plates carefully.

5   Mark never *makes* any trouble.

Some day, over the rainbow / **THE TIME IS <u>FUTURE</u>**

Write the *future* tense of each italicized verb.

1   They *called* their miniature collie "Minnie."

2   Bob *lost* the first round in the tournament.

3   Al *likes* to keep working all the time.

4   Pat *answers* the phone like a grownup.

5   Joe *saw* a movie full of action and suspense.

70

Here's How to Form the Past Tense

HOW DO <u>REGULAR VERBS</u> FORM THE PAST TENSE?

Most verbs add *ed* or *d* to form the past tense.

PRESENT:	walk	answer	pitch	loan
PAST:	walk*ed*	answer*ed*	pitch*ed*	loan*ed*
PRESENT:	bake	desire	care	love
PAST:	bake*d*	desire*d*	care*d*	love*d*

Hundreds of verbs follow this rule. Learn the endings: *ed* / *d*.

HOW DO <u>IRREGULAR VERBS</u> FORM THE PAST TENSE?

Instead of adding an ending (as above for regular verbs), irregular verbs change their spelling or use a different word.

PRESENT:	speak	go	see	do	eat
PAST:	spoke	went	saw	did	ate

Only about fifty verbs are "irregular," and you can use the handy list below to help you remember the past tense of these everyday verbs.

IRREGULAR VERBS

PRESENT	PAST	PRESENT	PAST
become	became	flee	fled
begin	began	fly	flew
blow	blew	forget	forgot
break	broke	freeze	froze
burst	burst	get	got
choose	chose	go	went
come	came	grow	grew
dive	dived	hang (clothing)	hung
do	did	hang (person)	hanged
draw	drew	know	knew
drink	drank	lay (put down)	laid
drive	drove	lead (guide)	led
eat	ate	lie (rest)	lay
fall	fell	lie (fib)	lied
fight	fought	raise (lift)	raised

IRREGULAR VERBS

PRESENT	PAST	PRESENT	PAST
rise (go up)	rose	steal	stole
run	ran	swim	swam
say	said	take	took
see	saw	teach	taught
set	set	tear (rip)	tore
sing	sang	throw	threw
sit	sat	wear	wore
speak	spoke	write	wrote

TROUBLESOME VERB FORMS

Memorize these twelve!

has begun	have gone
is broken	should have known
could have come	might have taken
should have done	should have seen
must have eaten	has rung
had fallen	could have thrown

Then try the sentences to test yourself on pages 73-74.

Set your watch back / **PAST TENSE**

Write the past tense of the verb that fits the meaning of the sentence.

1 When I was younger, I (**drink**) lots of milk.

2 Climbing over the fence, Tom (**tear**) his pants.

3 Vermont in winter was so cold, we almost (**freeze**) to death.

4 The strong wind (**break**) a branch off our tree.

5 The lie-detector test proved that he (**speak**) the truth.

6 Yesterday I (**write**) a letter to Barbara.

7 Last week we (**throw**) away the rubbish.

72

8   I have always (**say**) the truth about my friends.

9   The reporter described how they (**hang**) the criminal.

10 A young woman (**swim**) across the English Channel.

11 The police caught the man who (**steal**) the car.

12 The group all (**go**) to the movie last night.

13 They made a mistake when they (**run**) away from home.

14 Escape did not help because they (**take**) their problems with
    them anyway.

15 Last year she (**grow**) taller than her brother and sister.

16 Everybody (**see**) the circus in town last summer.

17 Looking in the oven, she saw she (**forget**) the cake.

18 The top layer (**get**) brown, almost burned.

19 We were so thirsty we (**drink**) a whole quart of milk.

20 The boxers (**fight**) right up to the last bell.

SOME SPECIAL VERB FORMS YOU HAVE TO MEMORIZE

As you learned (see page 72), some helping verbs are used together with a past participle. Example:

I *have seen* the Mets play.
(helping verb *have* + past participle *seen*)

The following verb forms are the most troublesome because
they are irregular.

1   It has *begun* to rain. (not *began*)

2   The glass is *broken*. (not *broke*)

3   You could have *come* earlier. (not *came*)

4 He should have *done* it himself. (not *did*)

5 We must have *eaten* a whole watermelon. (not *ate*)

6 She had *fallen* over a stool. (not *fell*)

7 They have *gone* home already. (not *went*)

8 You should have *known* the answer. (not *knew*)

9 We might have *taken* it by mistake. (not *took*)

10 You should have *seen* those acrobats. (not *saw*)

11 Has the recess bell *rung* yet? (not *rang*)

12 He could have *thrown* the ball higher. (not *threw*)

Know these / **VERB FORMS**

Using the past participle form, write the *past tense* of the verb to complete these sentences.

1 The balloon was *(break)* with a bang.

2 We should have *(go)* as soon as possible.

3 You should have *(see)* your friend in school.

4 She could not have *(do)* any better had she tried.

5 Although they had *(take)* the shortcut, we beat them home.

In This Lesson We Learned

The ***tense*** of the ***verb*** shows the *time* that the action takes place. There are three tenses: present, past, and future.

- Most verbs form the past tense by adding *ed* or *d*.
- The future tense uses *will* or *shall* as a helper.

74

WORD-STUDY USING VERBS

Verbs are among the most powerful words in our language because they show action and describe states of being. Verbs form the heart of a sentence because they tell what the subject does. Verbs also tell the time that something happens; whether past, present, or future. Therefore, you should increase your knowledge of verbs and how to use them.

EXERCISES

A   Write the verb in parentheses that has the *same meaning* as the italicized verb in each sentence below.

1   The letter-carrier *inquired* about the mail-box for the new tenant.
 (**asked, begged, demanded**)

2   Our tailor charges two dollars for service when he *alters* a skirt or a pair of pants.
 (**cleans, changes, presses**)

3   Smoke from chemical factories *pollutes* the air.
    (**warms, fouls, purifies**)

4   When armies cannot win wars, the leaders of their people
    negotiate terms for peace.
    (**discuss, refuse, betray**)

5   A thank-you note shows that you *appreciate* a favor received.
    (**ignore, accept, value**)

6   If anyone *loiters* in or near a school building, he trespasses.
    (**scribbles, idles, peddles**)

7   A kind judge may *grant* permission to lower the amount of
    bail to be set.
    (**allow, forbid, continue**)

8   Before you do anything to somebody else, you'd better *reflect*
    on the results.
    (**guess, forget, think**)

9   When a team fails to show up for a game, that team *forfeits*
    the game.
    (**wins, puts off, loses**)

10 Parents out of their great love for their children will forgive
    and not *condemn* their faults.
    (**blame, excuse, permit**)

B   Write the verb that fits the meaning and the number of missing letters indicated in parentheses.

1   The firecrackers **e (6) d** *(burst)* with a loud noise.

2   A moat filled with water **s (7) s** *(goes all around)* the castle.

3   Win or lose, it all **d (5) s** *(relies)* on you and the efforts you
    put forth.

4   On national holidays, we show love of country when we **d (5) y**
    (wave) our flag.

5   A soldier salutes an officer because Army rules **d (4) d** *(re-
    quire)* this sign of respect.

C Complete each sentence with a word selected from the verb list below.

parading	spurted
respond	mingle
declare	rebukes
impress	suspected
toured	provoke

1 He was showing off just to __?__ the girls.

2 The principal visited our class when he __?__ the building yesterday.

3 The store manager __?__ that one of the youngsters was shoplifting.

4 As our runner approached the finish line, he made a strong effort and __?__ to victory.

5 When questioned by a policeman, you must __?__ by giving your name and address.

6 If you leave your friends and __?__ with the crowd, you may get lost.

7 A harmless practical joke sometimes may __?__ trouble between two boys.

8 Every year at Atlantic City during the Miss America Contest, we see lovely girls __?__ across the stage.

9 When you return from a foreign country, you must __?__ to the customs officer the items in your baggage.

10 Are you able to accept it as graciously as possible when a grownup __?__ you for misbehaving?

D Write *S* for *same* and *O* for *opposite* in meaning.

1 admire / like
2 yield / surrender
3 waste / conserve
4 liquefy / solidify
5 tease / taunt
6 fasten / loosen
7 intake / outgo
8 challenge / defy
9 stray / wander
10 inhale / exhale

Only those ideas belong to you for which you know the right words.

E Action verbs are colorful, moving, picturesque. For example, when a superstar pitcher throws a baseball, they say it "pops," "burns," "hops," "skips," "jumps," "bams," "booms," "tails," "sails," "smokes," "swoops," "sinks," or "whooshes." Maybe some other batters would say that the ball seems to "curve," "slide," "swoosh," "dip," "dance," "hobble," "gallop," "bounce," "zing," "zap," and so on. These verbs show all kinds of action!

Add at least two more and different *action verbs* to each of these groups below. Use your imagination!

1 The wind *blew/whipped/buzzed/*across the waters of the bay.

2 The cat *meowed/screeched/wailed/*during the night.

3 The crowd *shouted/yelled/chanted/*for the winning team.

4 The motor *roared/purred/sputtered/*as it churned the lake water.

5 The baby *cried/whimpered/whined/*for attention in the crib.

6   The skater *whizzed/skidded/whirled/*along the ice rink.

7   The batter *hit/smashed/lobbed/*the ball into left field.

8   The singer *crooned/sang/hummed/*some favorite tunes.

9   The prisoner *begged/pleaded/prayed/*for mercy.

10 The quarterback *threw/tossed/lobbed/*a forward pass.

The larger the vocabulary you build up, the better able you become to refine your images and ideals.

PRONOUNS

Every day we use a couple of dozen small words in place of hundreds of names of persons, places, and things. These words are the most familiar ones you know; for example, *you* and *I*, *he* and *she*, *we* and *they*. Take the little word *it* which stands for thousands of things. You find these pronouns used everywhere; for example, in song titles, *"Me* and *my* shadow"; in the prayer, "Give *us* this day *our* daily bread"; in current slang phrases, "Sock *it* to *him!*"

★   Why do we use pronouns in place of nouns?

Read this passage with no pronouns and see why!

> Louis told Mary that Louis and Mary would practice tossing a football after supper. Mary told Louis that Louis and Mary could practice with Dad in the back yard of Dad, Louis, and Mary. Accidentally, Louis hit Mary in Mary's eye. Mary put ice on Mary's eye.

To avoid the needless repetition of names, use pronouns this way:

> Louis told Mary that *they* would practice tossing a football after supper. *She* told *him* that *they* could practice with Dad in *their* back yard. Accidentally, Louis hit Mary in *her* eye. *She* put ice on *her* eye.

Definition	Pronouns are words used in place of nouns in order to avoid repetition. They are shortcuts for names of persons, places, and things.

Pronouns streamline sentences by avoiding awkward repeating of names and things. See the sentences below for the better way of saying things.

1 POOR: The children were bored, so Mother took the children to the zoo.
　　　　　　　N.

BETTER: The children were bored, so Mother took them to the zoo.
　　　　　　　　　　　　　　　　　　　　　　　　　　　PRON.

2 POOR: Fred cannot play ball today because Fred injured Fred's arm.
　　　　　　　　　　　　　　　　　　　　　　N.
　　　　　　　N.

BETTER: Fred cannot play ball today because he injured his arm.
　　　　　　　　　　　　　　　　　　　　　　PRON.　　　PRON.

3 POOR: Father bought a gift for Helen and Mary and gave the gift to Helen and Mary on Sunday.
　　　　　　　N.　　　N.　　　　　N.

BETTER: Father bought a gift for Helen and Mary and gave it to them on Sunday.
PRON.　PRON.

First try / **SPOT THE PRONOUNS**

Write all the *pronouns* in these sentences.

1 When I sent the letter to you, I forgot to put your zip code on it.

2 We do not always do what is best for us, so our parents try to advise us for our good.

3 Will you please tell me when they intend to visit us?

4 If she asks you about me, tell her that I'm not at home.

5   They asked him to return their deposit because it was raining and they wanted to go home.

Answer these questions by replacing the blanks with *pronouns* that fit the meaning.

1   Do you have a nickname?

—?— have a nickname.

2   Who gave you your real name?

My parents gave —?— my real name.

3   Whose book is this?

This is —?— book.

4   Did you see Tom and Mary?

Yes, I saw —?— and —?—.

5   Is it day or night when the sun shines?

—?— is day when the sun shines.

Personal Pronouns

Personal pronouns refer to the speaker, to the person spoken to, or to the person spoken about.

These three persons may be singular (just one) or plural (more than one). For ready help, here is a list of these everyday personal pronouns arranged according to the way they are used.

	SINGULAR	PLURAL
FIRST PERSON *(the speaker)*	I, me, my, mine, myself	we, us, our, ours, ourselves
SECOND PERSON *(person spoken to)*	you, your, yours, yourself	you, your, yours, yourselves
THIRD PERSON *(person spoken about)*	he, him, his, himself, she, her, hers, herself	they, them, their, theirs, themselves

Think hard / **PERSONAL PRONOUNS IN SENTENCES**

Can you pick out the personal pronouns in these sentences? Write them on your answer sheet. Can you tell which person? Below each pronoun that you found, write *first* (for the speaker), *second* (for the person spoken to), and *third* (for the person spoken about). To show you how, the first sentence has been done for you.

1   I will show you how they settled the argument.
    first   **second**   **third**

2   Have you seen yourself in a mirror lately?

3   He gave her our best wishes on her birthday.

4   They did not know their way to your house.

5   Pick up only ours and leave theirs alone.

6   Just keep your hands off me, or we'll fight.

7   "You ought to be ashamed of yourselves!" he said.

8   "I will do that all by myself," she said.

9   Now is their turn to shake hands, not mine.

10   If you really mean that, let us be friends.

Impersonal Pronoun — It

How about the pronoun *it?* **It refers to nobody.** It is used everywhere to refer to any *place* or *thing*.

He dropped his shoe and picked *it* up.
The door hinge was squeaking, so we oiled *it*.
When the rain is heavy, *it* floods the street.
Can you lift *it?*
I'll do *it* all by myself.
Cool *it!*

Caution: it's = it is (Look how it's raining!)

Possessive Pronouns

Possessive pronouns are words used to show ownership. They tell you whom a thing belongs to, without giving the name of the person. For example, notice these questions and answers:

Q. Mary, is this *your* wallet?
A. No, that one is not *mine*.

Q. Can everybody fit in Louis' sports car?
A. If they squeeze in, they can all get in *his* car.

Study the list below.

S I N G U L A R {	my, mine your, yours his her, hers its	P L U R A L {	our, ours your, yours their theirs
			Notice! No apostrophe!

Caution! **Since possessive pronouns show ownership, they never need an apostrophe.** For example, keep the spelling as shown in the list above:

This land is *ours*. (not our's or ours')
Which house is *theirs?* (not their's or theirs')

Write the answers to these questions using possessive pronouns.

1 Is this your seat?

2 Who owns that rowboat?

3 Why did they fence in the back yard?

4 Whose cousins came to visit?

5 Why do hotels label the towels?

6 How much belongs to each one of them?

7 What happened to the muffler of the car?

8 Why do the boys cheer for the team?

9 How can the girls find the right skates?

10 Will you chip in for the special collection?

How Can You Avoid Errors in Using Pronouns?

Where are the trouble spots in using pronouns? There are two kinds of mistakes or stumbling blocks which you must learn to avoid:

A SPELLING BLUNDERS	**CORRECT WAY**
1 The fur coat lost *it's* shine.	its
2 Is that book *your's*?	yours
3 Yes, it is *our's!*	ours
4 He almost drowned *hisself*.	himself
5 They decided to do it *theirselves*.	themselves

B WRONG WAY

	WRONG WAY	CORRECT WAY
1	*Us* two boys went fishing.	We
2	Let's you and *I* be friends.	me
3	Give the same to him and *I*.	me
4	Dorothea looks taller than *me*.	I
5	Keep this secret between you and *I*.	me

Errors can be costly.

CORRECTING ERRORS IN PRONOUNS

Write the correct form of the pronoun to fit each sentence.

1   This comes to you from Mother and *(I, me)* with love.

2   When we checked the luggage, we found one of *(ours, our's)*.

3   Let's you and *(me, I)* shake hands and forget the whole thing.

4   Are you sure it was *(I, me)* who broke the ice?

5   Why don't we invite Tom, Stanley, and *(he, him)* next time?

6   Everybody seemed happy there except *(she, her)* and her sister.

7   Thank goodness it wasn't *(them, they)* in the wrecked car.

8   Answer the phone and see whether it is *(she, her)*, please!

9   If *(it's, its)* Barbara, tell her we'll see her soon.

10 Now it happens to be *(yours, your's)* this time.

11 How can they hurt *(theirselves, themselves)* with these toys?

12 He dropped the sound box with *(its, it's)* windup key.

13 I guess it was *(he, him)* who told the dean the whole story.

14 What's it to *(him, he)* whether the facts support his alibi?

15 As a shopper, Mother is much shrewder than *(me, I)*.

16 She looks at quality and price as you and *(I, me)* should do.

17 On the way home, I sat between *(he, him)* and her.

18 It must have been *(him, he)* who left the message.

19 Pick up the marbles; they're all *(yours, your's)*.

20 If these are not actually ours, then they must be *(theirs, their's)*.

FOR EXTRA CREDIT

Write 10 sentences using some of the pronouns you have learned in this lesson. Underline each pronoun and be ready to tell whether it is singular, plural, personal, impersonal, or possessive.

Master these / **CORRECT FORMS OF PRONOUNS**

Write the correct form of the *pronoun* in parentheses.

1 The new skates belong to *(her, she)*.

2 When the suit is ready, it will be delivered to *(us, we)* at home.

3 Despite complaints, it is *(we, us)* taxpayers who pay for foreign aid.

4 The bride chose Valerie, Margaret, and *(she, her)* as brides-maids.

5 Ruth looked as rosy and happy as *(her, she)* was at Paul's wedding.

6 In this situation, *(us, we)* fellows must stay together.

7 Can you throw a baseball as fast as *(he, him)*?

8 When I see her smiling, I feel as glad as *(her, she)* too.

9 The brown paint on the siding showed *(its, it's)* blisters in the sun.

10 At last, we can say one of *(our's, ours)* won the medal.

Story / **A VISIT TO GRANDMOTHER**

Re-write the following paragraph, substituting *pronouns* for persons, places, and things mentioned.

John and Donna went to Donna's grandmother's house. Grand-mother served John and Donna sandwiches and soda with cake and fruit at Grandmother's house. Then John and Donna phoned Lee and Peter to invite Lee and Peter over for a game of cards. Lee and Peter told Donna that Lee and Peter would be glad to join John and Donna in a little while. John, Donna, Lee, Peter, and Grandmother played for fun, using pennies. Grandmother put all the pennies back in Grandmother's cookie jar at the end.

> **In This Lesson We Learned**
>
> *Pronouns* are used in place of nouns to avoid repetition of names of persons, places, and things. Pronouns take no apostrophe to show possession.

PRONOUNS WHO/THAT/ WHICH

Three little words very often used as pronouns are *who, that,* and *which.* They have special uses as follows:

| WHO | refers to persons |

The boy *who* raised his hand first may answer.
person

| THAT | refers to persons or things or animals |

The girl *that* sits near the door goes out first.
person

The book *that* I borrowed I will return now.
thing

| WHICH | refers to things and animals |

The building *which* faces the East River is the U.N.
thing

This is the dog *which* bit me.
animal

MEMORIZE THIS BOX!

who	→	person		
that	→	person / thing / animal		
which	→		thing / animal	

NOTE WELL!

WHICH never refers to persons! It may be used only with animals and things.

WRONG: The man *which* just came in is my father.
RIGHT: The man *who* (or *that*) just came in is my father.

THAT is correct in every situation where you wish to use it.

RIGHT: The fence *that* goes around the farm is just a careful pile of stones.
RIGHT: The dog *that* bit the lady is being tested for rabies.
RIGHT: The hero *that* got the medal was a marine.

Target for today! / **USING WHO, THAT, WHICH CORRECTLY**

Write the pronoun *(who, that,* or *which)* that fits the meaning in each sentence.

1 Tom is my neighbor __?__ will enter college next year.

2 The skirt __?__ Mary chose is the more expensive one.

3 The country __?__ borders the United States on the south is Mexico.

4 There goes the fellow __?__ honks his horn to say hello.

5 Opposite the bank there is a gas station __?__ sells gas five cents less on a gallon.

6   I wonder __?__ way takes less time—by motorcycle or by speedboat?

7   I like a tree __?__ gives fruit as well as shade.

8   Do you know __?__ invented the electric light bulb?

9   The farmer gave us the biggest tomato __?__ we have ever seen.

10 The store __?__ satisfies the customers does more business.

Spot the errors / **CORRECT THE PRONOUNS**

Some of these sentences are correct as they stand. Write *C* on your answer sheet. Spot an incorrect pronoun and correct the error by substituting another pronoun for the italicized one.

1   Is she the teacher *which* just got married?

2   Is that the camera *which* you got for your birthday?

3   The Bronx Zoo has the largest elephant *who* was ever placed in captivity.

4   The man who came to dinner was the one *that* stayed after breaking his leg.

5   The newspaper *who* prints the truth may get more subscribers.

6   The Governor accused the leaders *which* started the riot.

7   Having appeared in movies and television for many years, Lassie is the dog *which* we know best.

8   Give this to the girl *who* has the best attendance.

9   The crowds backed away from the cage because of the lion *who* was roaring for raw meat.

10   This antique ship's writing desk used to belong to one of the men *which* built the railroads to the West.

Sentences that swing along / **USE WHO, THAT, WHICH IN SENTENCES**

Write sentences using the pronouns *who, that,* or *which* in the situations suggested below.

1   The President *who*

2   The nation *which*

3   A problem *that*

4   Take one of these costumes *which*

5   Try a hat *that*

6   Ask the lady *who*

7   The captain of the squad *that*

8   The member of the club *who*

9   The falls flow down to the river *which*

10   Our neighbor's dog *which*

In This Lesson We Learned

The pronouns *who, that,* and *which* refer to persons, things, or animals according to the special uses listed on page 89.

ADJECTIVES

An *adjective* is a word used to tell us something about a noun.

An adjective may answer these questions:

WHAT KIND?	HOW MUCH?	HOW MANY?
small boy	*ten* cents	*few* students
red apple	*five* pounds	*many* girls
young lady	*four* dollars	*some* peaches

Adjectives at Work

Take a look at some adjectives of color, size, shape, number, etc., when used with nouns in sentences. What do they tell you about the nouns?

$\qquad\qquad\qquad$ N. $\qquad\qquad\qquad$ N.

1 A *big American* flag flies in front of *our* school.

ADJECTIVES		NOUNS
A	tells the number of	flags
big	tells the size of	flag
American	tells the kind of	flag
our	tells the owner of	school

2   *That strong* **N.** boy carried *this heavy* **N.** package.

ADJECTIVES		NOUNS
That	tells which one of	boys
strong	tells what kind of	boy
this	tells which one of	packages
heavy	tells what kind of	package

3   *Several* **N.** girls were talking about *the basketball* **N.** game.

ADJECTIVES		NOUNS
Several	tells how many of	girls
the	tells how many of	games
basketball	tells what kind of	game

4   *Two thick* **N.** nickels are equal to *one slim* **N.** dime.

ADJECTIVES		NOUNS
Two	tells how many of the	nickels
thick	tells the size of the	nickels
one	tells how many of the	dimes
slim	tells the size of the	dime

Note: The small words *a / an / the* used as adjectives (meaning "one") are called *articles* and may be bypassed in this discussion.

Positions of Adjectives

You are used to seeing adjectives **in front of nouns.**

> a *cold* drink
> a *tall* building
> a *close* call

Sometimes you find them **trailing after the nouns.**

> a boy, *big* and *strong*
> the message, *short* and *sweet*
> the ending, *unbelievable* but *true*

Another position you may spot is **after a linking verb,** which really connects the subject with the adjective.

The sky is *blue.*
The sea looks *calm.*
This apple tastes *good.*

To help you remember these different ways of using adjectives in your own speaking and writing, take a long look at this brief box.

POSITIONS OF ADJECTIVES

before the noun	— our *old* car
after the noun	— our car, *old* and *dirty*
after a linking verb	— our car is *old*

Just a quick refresher about the "linking verb," discussed on page 60. **A linking verb is a verb of being or of the senses. It connects the subject with the following word.** Here are some sentences showing how adjectives follow verbs.

Kathy appears sunburned.
S.   L.V.   ADJ.

Loretta looks hungry.
S.   L.V.   ADJ.

This paper feels smooth.
S.   L.V.   ADJ.

Burning leaves smell sharp.
S.   L.V.   ADJ.

A driver on the highway must be alert.
S.   L.V. ADJ.

What's a linking verb?

In the spotlight today / **ADJECTIVES MODIFY NOUNS**

Pick out the adjective and write the noun that it modifies or describes. Disregard the articles: *a, an, the.*

EXAMPLE: The *little* boy found a *lucky* dollar.

1   Africa offers a great variety of natural wonders.

2   This vast continent holds many surprises for the visitor.

3   The lush jungles are filled with incredible wildlife.

4 The Congo River is a golden track through the green forests.

5 The diamond mines, rich and secret, hold buried treasure.

6 The tourist resorts combine ancient traditions and modern history.

7 Many former colonies have become free nations.

8 Unusual sculptures have influenced living artists.

9 Travelers carry movie cameras instead of deadly rifles.

10 Africa, dark and unknown, has become a new exciting land.

A smooth start / **WRITING ADJECTIVES**

Answer these questions by writing appropriate adjectives in place of the blanks.

1 What colors are the grass and the sky?

The grass is __?__ and the sky is __?__.

2 How many legs has a newborn puppy?

A newborn puppy has __?__ legs.

3 What kind of taste does sugar have?

Sugar has a __?__ taste.

4 Does a giraffe have a short neck?

A giraffe has an unusually __?__ neck.

5 At which meal do we generally have cereal?

Cereal is a __?__ food.

Proper Adjectives

Some adjectives must be spelled with a capital letter because they are formed from proper nouns that are used to describe a particular person, place, or thing. For example, compare the nouns with their adjectives in the following list; notice the change in spelling to form the adjectives.

PROPER NOUNS	PROPER ADJECTIVES	
England	English	(muffins)
France	French	(toast)
Italy	Italian	(airlines)
Scotland	Scotch	(whiskey)
China	Chinese	(fortune cookies)
Ireland	Irish	(linen)
Greece	Greek	(temples)
Africa	African	(tribes)
Russia	Russian	(ballet)
Spain	Spanish	(wine)

Review proper nouns on page 35.

Help your writing! / **WRITING PROPER ADJECTIVES**

Write the proper adjective that comes from the noun given in parentheses.

1 Ladies' dresses are designed by (Rome) and (Paris) fashion experts.

2 Have you ever bought a (Switzerland) watch or a piece of (Mexico) silver?

3 We once visited the (Canada) side of Niagara Falls, and we met some people speaking the (France) language.

4 I have a pen pal who writes (Japan) letters with some (America) words and expressions sprinkled in between.

5 (Germany) beer and (Poland) ham are popular imports.

97

Write sentences using the italicized *adjectives* in the phrases given below.

1 a *red* light

2 a *telephone* ring

3 a *television* program

4 *nine* players

5 *twelve* eggs

FOR EXTRA CREDIT

Take a good look at someone in the room and write a brief description using any of these and other *adjectives:*

tall	dull	chubby
short	interesting	slim
smiling	attentive	busy
grumpy	dreamy	lazy
tidy	pale	serious
messy	tanned	funny
quiet	quick	tired
talkative	slow	active

Comparing Adjectives

When you go to a wedding ceremony, you hear the couple agreeing to take each other "for richer or poorer, for better or worse." Sometimes you see two youngsters standing up straight while arguing, "I'm taller than you!" Or you may see a couple splashing in a pool, saying, "I can swim faster than you!"

richer / poorer   taller / shorter

better / worse   faster / slower

These eight adjectives are said to be in the **comparative degree**. This means that two persons, places, or things are placed together in order to find which one has more or less of a certain ability or quality. The one that is superior is tall-*er*, rich-*er*, fast-*er*, etc.

Now, let's go a step further and put three or more persons or things together. Student *A* works hard; Student *B* works harder; Student *C* works hardest. One of these is rated the highest because he works hardest. Take a hero sandwich six inches long; another hero sandwich may be longer by two inches; and a third hero sandwich may be the longest of all. Once again, you notice which is tops. The one that is the best of all is shown by the ending: long-*est*, hard-*est*, rich-*est*, etc.

The eight adjectives below are said to be in the **superlative degree**.

      strongest / weakest   biggest / smallest

      youngest / oldest   hottest / coldest

There are two easy rules for remembering how to compare adjectives. You probably know them already. Memorize!

I   **Adjectives of *one* syllable add *er* or *est*.**

   old   →   old*er*   →   old*est*
   young →   young*er* →   young*est*

II **Adjectives of *more than one* syllable use *more* or *most*.**

   beautiful   →   *more* beautiful   →   *most* beautiful
   bighearted →   *more* bighearted →   *most* bighearted

Some adjectives can be compared either way; as you like it.

      clever →   { cleverer or more clever
                 { cleverest or most clever

      hungry →   { hungrier or more hungry
                 { hungriest or most hungry

However, you must NEVER use both *more* and *er*, or *most* and *est*, for the same comparison.

WRONG:

the *more cleverer* man

the *most cleverest* man

RIGHT:

the *more clever* man,
or the *cleverer* man

the *most clever* man,
or the *cleverest* man

SPECIAL WORDS

There are just a few everyday words that *do not* follow the rules. You must learn these by heart!

POSITIVE	COMPARATIVE	SUPERLATIVE
good	better	best
bad	worse	worst
little	less	least
much	more	most
some	more	most
many	more	most

Hit the bull's eye / **COMPARING ADJECTIVES**

Write the missing adjectives for the *positive, comparative,* and *superlative* degrees.

POSITIVE	COMPARATIVE	SUPERLATIVE
1 cold	__?__	__?__
2 __?__	hotter	__?__
3 brown	__?__	__?__
4 __?__	__?__	greenest
5 fat	__?__	__?__

6	_?_	lovelier	_?_
7	smart	_?_	_?_
8	_?_	_?_	most interesting
9	_?_	better	_?_
10	_?_	_?_	worst

FOR EXTRA CREDIT

Write 5 sentences using any of the different *adjectives* given above. Try to describe a person, a place, or a thing that you are familiar with.

Show some muscle / **WRITE COMPARISONS OF ADJECTIVES**

Complete the following sentences by writing the correct form of the word given in parentheses. Example:

An electric toaster works *(fast)* than a coal stove.

An electric toaster works FASTER than a coal stove.

1 Matthew is the *(short)* of the two children.

2 This summer's storms seem *(bad)* than last year's.

3 Which do you like *(good)*, movies or TV shows?

4 When you do it yourself, the job seems a bit *(easy)* to finish.

5 Do you think his watch is *(reliable)* than mine?

6 Which of the two cars sells *(cheap)*?

7 These pickles taste *(sour)* than the ones we ate yesterday.

8 With exercise, your muscles will grow *(strong)* than his.

9 Thin the paint by adding more turpentine and *(little)* enamel.

10 A hundred-watt bulb shines *(bright)* than a forty-watt bulb.

Choose wisely / **ADJECTIVES COMPARED**

Choose the correct comparison for each sentence below. Write the letter *A* or *B* on your answer paper.

1 Stanley seems —?— of the two fellows.

   (A) the taller   *(B)* the tallest

2 Mary swimming alongside Kathy went —?— across the pool.

   (A) more faster   *(B)* faster

3 The neighbor's car ran so smoothly because the engine was —?— than our old Chevrolet.

   (A) newer   *(B)* more newer

4 Last night's TV show was —?— all summer because of the stale jokes.

   (A) the baddest   *(B)* the worst

5 When he opened the mail and found a check, he was the —?— man on the block.

   (A) most happiest   *(B)* happiest

6 In spite of the medicine, his toothache felt —?— until the dentist pulled the tooth out.

   (A) worse   *(B)* worst

7 The church bells sounded __?__ echoing across the meadow early in the morning.

   (A) sadder   (B) more sadder

8 If you draw a sketch of your bedroom, it will make it a little __?__ to see the layout.

   (A) more clearer   (B) clearer

9 Mother makes Italian meatballs —?— by using a fragrant herb for flavoring.

   (A) more spicy   (B) more spicier

10 Who is __?__, your brother or your sister?

   (A) smarter   (B) smartest

In This Lesson We Learned

Adjectives are words used to describe nouns. They tell us "what kind" of person, place, or thing.

- Use *er* or *est* for comparing adjectives of one syllable.
- Use *more* or *most* for adjectives longer than one syllable.

WORD-STUDY USING ADJECTIVES

In all word-study,
make it your business to
learn not only the meaning
but also the proper
use of words, so that you may
grow in <u>vocabulary</u>
and <u>intelligence</u>.

Adjectives are words used to add color, size, shape, etc., to nouns that stand for people, places, and things. You know how often you use them, or see them in ads, or read them in the daily newspaper.

Get your *cold* drinks!

Here's the *latest* news.

Fly the *friendly* skies.

Our *family* doctor.

A *tough* policeman.

Adjectives build atmosphere or local color in a story.

> In the days of the *wild* and *woolly* west.
>
> On the *quiet* banks of the Potomac River.
>
> The *drizzling* rain fell on the *shining* pavement.

You, too, can use colorful adjectives to brighten your own themes or letters to your friends.

EXERCISES

A Write the adjectives, selected from the list, that complete the sentences below. Do not use the same word more than once!

ADJECTIVES

slippery	quickest	polluted
helpful	useful	thoughtful
brief	empty	salty
finer	glad	amazing
ordinary	important	truthful

1 Roasted peanuts with a —?— taste make one thirsty.

2 Water, air, and all around us are becoming —?— and unsafe.

3 "Nothing could be —?— than to be in Carolina in the morning."

4 Because of the ice, the sidewalk was too —?— for comfort.

5 The magician's tricks were so —?— that everybody clapped.

6 Sometimes the longest way around is really the —?— way home.

7 The life story of a hero may be different from an —?— man's.

8 The story tells how Ali Baba hid himself in an —?— jar.

9   A sad heart tires in a mile; but a ___?___ heart goes all the way.

10   George Washington stands as a model of a ___?___ youngster.

B   Which adjectives are the same in meaning? Which ones are opposite in meaning? Write **S** = *same* or **O** = *opposite*.

EXAMPLES: quiet   /   noisy   =   **O**
            brittle /   fragile =   **S**

1	ugly	/	beautiful	6	wonderful	/	terrible
2	broken	/	burst	7	lovely	/	hateful
3	dim	/	vague	8	gigantic	/	monstrous
4	stingy	/	miserly	9	noble	/	grand
5	careful	/	reckless	10	generous	/	grasping

C   Write a sentence using each adjective below.

1   delicious   4   vanishing

2   unusual   5   surprising

3   grateful

The better you distinguish between shades of word meanings, the more precise grows your expression of ideas.

ADVERBS

WHAT ARE ADVERBS?

Watch the answers to the following questions as you read them aloud:

QUESTIONS	ANSWERS
When will the next bus come?	*Soon.*
Where are you going now?	*Home.*
How do your guppies breed?	*Quickly.*

These answers are all called adverbs because they modify <u>verbs.</u>

The next bus will <u>come</u> *soon.*
            V.   **ADV.**

(*soon* = adverb of time modifying *will come*)

I am <u>going</u> *home* now.
  V.   **ADV.**

(*home* = adverb of place modifying *am going*)

My guppies <u>breed</u> *quickly.*
       V.   **ADV.**

(*quickly* = adverb of manner modifying *breed*)

Now, let's look at another kind of job that adverbs can do. Besides the use of adverbs to say something about *verbs,* you can use adverbs to say something about adjectives. These adverbs answer the question *How much?* or *How little?*

QUESTIONS	ANSWERS
Do you feel glad today?	*Very.*
Were you tired yesterday?	*Somewhat.*
Are your shoes worn-out?	*Slightly.*

2

These words are called adverbs because they modify adjectives.

I feel *very* glad today.
ADV. ADJ.

(How glad? *very*)

I was *somewhat* tired yesterday.
ADV.   ADJ.

(How tired? *somewhat*)

My shoes are *slightly* worn-out.
ADV.   ADJ.

(How worn-out? *slightly*)

3

There is a third use of adverbs; namely, to modify other adverbs.

We sang *so* happily at the party.
ADV. ADV.

(How happily? *so*)

She was *too* sadly downcast.
ADV. ADV.

(How sadly? *too*)

We became friends *quite* easily.
ADV. ADV.

(How easily? *quite*)

ADVERB + VERB Mary <u>often plays</u> the piano. 　　　ADV. + V. **ADVERB + ADJECTIVE** Tony is one of my <u>very best</u> friends. 　　　ADV. + ADJ. **ADVERB + ADVERB** My swimsuit was <u>only slightly</u> wet. 　　　ADV. + ADV.	**Definition** Adverbs are words used to modify (1) a verb, (2) an adjective, or (3) another adverb.

Make this a home run / **ADVERBS IN ACTION**

Pick out the adverb and write the verb, adjective, or adverb it modifies. Think of the questions *when? where? how?* (20 right = a home run!)

The adverb may be found in different positions in a sentence.

a After the verb: He came *late.*

b At the beginning of the sentence: *Suddenly* he sat down.

c Between the parts of a verb phrase: She has *often* called me.

MODIFYING A VERB

1 He opened the door slowly.

2 They saved their money and traveled abroad.

3 Silently, the cat stalked her prey.

4 Hopefully, she looked in the mailbox for a letter.

5 Small children have always been spoiled by grandparents.

MODIFYING AN ADJECTIVE

6 It was too good to be true.

7   After the explanation, we felt more confused.

8   Rubbing the ointment on the ankle made the pain less acute.

9   Her red dress looked slightly wrinkled.

10   Your welcome smile makes me very glad.

MODIFYING AN ADVERB

11   Some teenagers dress somewhat shabbily and in poor taste.

12   The painting on the wall seemed just slightly tilted.

13   You can straighten it quite easily.

14   My brother used to tell stories so vividly we believed them.

15   They left the parking lot rather hurriedly.

MODIFYING VERB, ADJECTIVE, OR ADVERB

16   She gave her time cheerfully as a "candy striper" in the hospital.

17   He stumbled and fell accidentally.

18   Have you never eaten a delicious mango?

19   Strange fruits are quite expensive.

20   The scooter was going too fast to stop.

Drive to centerfield / **WRITE SOME "LY" ADVERBS**

How can you spot an adverb?

Many adverbs end in **ly**. Here are a few samples. Can you think of others? Add 10 more.

rapidly	easily	hurriedly
slowly	readily	peacefully
hastily	specially	angrily
promptly	hungrily	quietly
cheerfully	occasionally	accidentally
hopefully	neatly	humbly
excitedly	shabbily	proudly
dizzily	secretly	merrily
jokingly	terribly	noisily
seriously	anxiously	gracefully

FOR EXTRA CREDIT

Write ten sentences using some of the adverbs in the above list.

How is your store of words? / **WRITING OTHER ADVERBS**

Some adverbs do not end in **ly**. Here are a few examples. Add 5 more.

not	here	later
too	there	soon
very	up	then
quite	down	before
somewhat	now	after

FOR EXTRA CREDIT
Write ten sentences using some of the adverbs in the previous list.

Comparing Adverbs

HOW DO YOU COMPARE ADVERBS?

You compare adverbs the same way as adjectives. You may take a look at pages 98-100 to see how it's done.

[A] REGULAR ADVERBS

Take some ordinary adverbs and arrange them like this to show how you can tell the difference in rate or degree, going up or going down the scale.

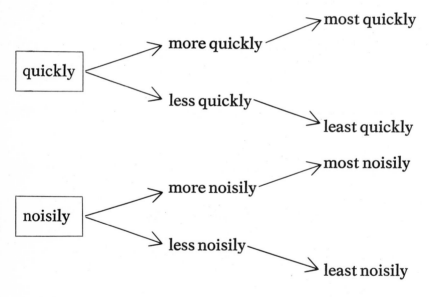

Some sentences will make these comparisons clearer.

An elephant moves through the jungle *more noisily* and *less quickly* than a tiger.

A jet plane takes off *more quickly* and *more noisily* than a propeller-driven plane.

Other adverbs show the change in rate or degree by using *er* and *est* at the end of the simple adverb.

$$near \rightarrow nearer \rightarrow nearest$$
$$soon \rightarrow sooner \rightarrow soonest$$

The *sooner* you come, the *nearer* you will be to the door.
The boy standing *nearest* the door gets out *soonest*.

B | IRREGULAR ADVERBS

As children grow up, they become *better* behaved and *less* troublesome.

> *Better behaved* is a step higher than *well behaved!*
> *Less troublesome* is a step lower than *troublesome!*

Let's see how they go UP or DOWN.

Some irregular adverbs are compared as follows:

POSITIVE	COMPARATIVE	SUPERLATIVE
far	farther	farthest
little	less	least
some	more	most
well	better	best

A few irregular adverbs are not compared. Examples: *always, never, no, not, sometimes, rarely, scarcely*, etc.

HERE'S HOW! We compare adverbs ...

POSITIVE	COMPARATIVE	SUPERLATIVE
(adverb)	**-er**	**-est**
Example: early	earlier	earliest
(adverb)	**more**	**most**
Example: daringly	more daringly	most daringly
(adverb)	**less**	**least**
Example: swiftly	less swiftly	least swiftly

**COMPARATIVE AND SUPERLATIVE
DEGREES OF ADVERBS**

Pick out the adverb and write the comparative and superlative forms.

1 He swings hard during the practice period before games.

2 To build muscles you must exercise regularly.

3 Theodore Roosevelt said, "Speak softly and carry a big stick."

4 If you eat sparingly, you will not become overweight.

5 Although he eats slowly, he manages to clean his plate.

6 If everybody enters the room quietly, the lesson can begin.

7 The end of the detour is near.

8 Our neighbor said the trees were close to his flowers and loudly objected.

9 We gave him some early blooming tomatoes as a friendly gesture.

10 Goodwill is more important than fences between neighbors.

A few tips / **ADVERBS ANSWER WHEN? WHERE? HOW?**

Three questions answered by adverbs are *when? where? how?*

EXAMPLES:

when?	Please come inside *immediately.*
where?	Just leave your wet boots *outside.*
how?	He crept *cautiously* up the steps.

Write the answers to the questions below using adverbs that show the time, or the place, or the way something is done.

1 How often do the tides rise and fall at the beach?

2 Where do you seek shelter when it rains outdoors?

3 How do you prefer your hamburger grilled?

4 When the telephone rings, how do you answer?

5 At the end of the game, how does the winning side cheer?

6 The batter swung fast but missed the ball. Why?

7 When did your brother get his hair trimmed?

8 Where do submarines cruise undetected?

9 How does a cedarwood closet smell?

10 How do you make your bed before leaving for school?

Let's go. / **COMPARING ADVERBS**

Write the missing adverbs for the blanks below.

POSITIVE	COMPARATIVE	SUPERLATIVE
1 rapidly	more rapidly	__?__
2 __?__	more slowly	most slowly
3 carefully	__?__	most carefully
4 evenly	more evenly	__?__
5 abruptly	more abruptly	__?__
6 gently	__?__	most gently
7 somewhat	__?__	most

8	__?__	sooner	soonest
9	well	__?__	best
10	badly	worse	__?__

Avoid Confusing Adverbs With Adjectives

Since some adverbs and adjectives look alike and some pupils grow careless, you find at times an adjective forced to do the work of an adverb. Examples:

✗ WRONG: Isn't she a *real* nice friend?

✓ RIGHT: Isn't she a *really* nice friend?

(*really* is an adverb modifying the adjective *nice*)

✗ WRONG: Yes, and she plays the piano very *good*.

✓ RIGHT: Yes, and she plays the piano very *well*.

(*well* is an adverb modifying the verb *plays*)

Avoid confusing adverbs with adjectives! Remember: an *adjective* modifies a noun; an *adverb* modifies a verb, an adjective, or another adverb.

1 RIGHT: I hope to see you *really* soon. (not *real*)

(adverb *really* modifies adverb *soon*)

2 RIGHT: Her dress looks *really* pretty. (not *real*)

(adverb *really* modifies adjective *pretty*)

3 RIGHT: Louis plays the guitar as *well* as Vincent. (not *good*)

(adverb *well* modifies verb *plays*)

4 RIGHT: Burnt toast smells *smoky*. (not *smokily*)

(adjective *smoky* modifies noun *toast*)

5 RIGHT: Eric scored *well* in the golf tournament. (not *good*)
(adverb *well* modifies verb *scored*)

6 RIGHT: Diet soda tastes too *sweet* for me. (not *sweetly*)
(adjective *sweet* modifies noun *soda*)

7 RIGHT: When he loses a game, he acts *badly*. (not *bad*)
(adverb *badly* modifies verb *acts*)

8 RIGHT: He shakes hands *coldly* and *limply*. (not *cold, limp*)
(adverbs *coldly* and *limply* modify verb *shakes*)

9 RIGHT: With my new glasses I can see very *well*. (not *good*)
(adverb *well* modifies verb *see*)

10 RIGHT: He caught on to the trick pretty *quickly*. (not *quick*)
(adverb *quickly* modifies verb *caught*)

Choose correctly / **ADJECTIVES OR ADVERBS?**

Choose the correct word in each sentence below. Write it on your answer paper.

1 These fresh flowers smell (**sweet** or **sweetly**).

2 I like Christa because she smiles so (**happily** or **happy**).

3 We all became acquainted quite (**easily** or **easy**).

4 Some tobacco smoke smells more (**fragrant** or **fragrantly**).

5 Milk is (**good** or **well**) for building teeth and bones in youngsters.

6 Gale sang pretty (**good** or **well**) last night.

7 You're going to feel better (**real** or **really**) soon.

117

8 The broken gate swung (**loosely** or **loose**) on its hinges.

9 Martha danced fast and (**gaily** or **gay**) to the bongo band.

10 Bob sat at the table staring (**sad** or **sadly**) into a cup of tea.

All hits, no errors / **ADJECTIVES OR ADVERBS?**

Write the word which makes the sentence correct.

1 The old piano in the attic doesn't play *(good, well)*.

2 He said he was *(sure, surely)* glad to be home again.

3 At the assembly, Dorothea spoke very *(good, well)*.

4 Home-cooked food looks and tastes *(delicious, deliciously)*.

5 Please answer these questions *(carefully, careful)*.

6 On account of the ice and fog, we *(nearly, near)* lost our way.

7 Bob used to play the guitar quite *(badly, bad)*.

8 John ate *(most, almost)* all of the cookies by himself.

9 Carmela plays tennis rather *(well, good)*.

10 Tom doesn't swim as *(good, well)* as his brother.

11 Examples in arithmetic must be done *(accurate, accurately)*.

12 Nino listened to the recording of music *(attentively, attentive)*.

13 A silk skirt feels slippery and *(smooth, smoothly)*.

14 He walked downstairs a bit too *(hurriedly, hurried)* and fell.

15 After the storm, the river rushed *(strong, strongly)* down the slope.

16 With a new coat of paint, our house looks *(beautiful, beautifully)*.

17 In the darkness all noises sounded *(strange, strangely)* to us.

18 You look sloppy when you dress *(carelessly, careless)*.

19 Seeing the broken vase, Mother appeared very *(angry, angrily)*.

20 Our TV set has been working rather *(poorly, poor)* lately.

For sharpshooters / **ADJECTIVES OR ADVERBS?**

Write the correct expression to fit each sentence below.

1 The heavy rain loosened the slope, making the earth slide down (gradual, gradually) to the bottom.

2 To escape, he dashed (quick, quickly) through the door.

3 His wounded leg hurt quite (badly, bad) as he ran.

4 The traffic moved very (slow, slowly) during the storm.

5 A police siren sounded (alarmingly, alarming) close at hand.

6 Kathy can paint landscapes (beautiful, beautifully) in oils.

7 With a few lessons, she could be pretty (well, good) at it.

8 The piece of material felt somewhat (rough, roughly) to touch.

119

9   At that bargain table, the prices were too (cheaply, cheap) to believe.

10 After the summer, we felt (eager, eagerly) to return home.

In This Lesson We Learned

- *Adverbs* are words used to modify a *verb,* an *adjective,* or another *adverb.* Avoid confusing adverbs with adjectives; adjectives describe *nouns.*

- Adverbs are compared like adjectives. You add *er/est,* or use the words *more/most* to show higher degrees and *less/ least* for lower degrees.

Slight differences do matter.

WORD-STUDY
USING ADVERBS

Words are like money in the bank: the more you have, the more you can spend!

Since adverbs are often used to say something about verbs, some adverbs show how the action takes place. They tell us the way things are being done and the time they occur. Thus, they help to round out the meaning. They are worth knowing and using. When used to modify adjectives or other adverbs, they tell us *how much* or *how little* of a certain quality or condition.

EXERCISES

A. Can you think of the *opposite* for each pair of words below? In parentheses you will find the number of missing letters.

1	here	/	t (3) e	(at a distance)
2	sooner	/	l (3) r	(at another time)
3	quietly	/	n (5) y	(with greater sound)
4	sadly	/	h (5) y	(with more joy)
5	very	/	s (6) t	(a little bit)
6	slowly	/	r (5) y	(quickly)

7	humbly	/	p (5) y	(feeling "puffed up")
8	sloppily	/	n (4) y	(with care and tidiness)
9	bitterly	/	s (5) y	(kindly, gently)
10	carefully	/	r (8) y	(wildly, with no concern)

B Spot the *one* word that does *not* mean the same as the rest of the words on the line. Write the word.

1 sometimes / occasionally / never / often /

2 truly / falsely / actually / really /

3 richly / wealthily / poorly / fabulously /

4 strongly / weakly / feebly / frailly /

5 damply / moistly / humidly / drily /

6 bravely / boldly / timidly / courageously /

7 idly / lazily / busily / laggingly /

8 reliably / dependably / faithfully / doubtfully /

9 scantily / skimpily / meagerly / amply /

10 warmly / icily / frigidly / coldly /

C Write a sentence using each adverb given below.

1 nervously

4 accidentally

2 patiently

5 always

3 naturally

D We form *adjectives* by adding certain endings to nouns, such as *able, al, ible, ful*.

EXAMPLE: hope + ful = hope*ful*
N.   ADJ.

We form *adverbs* by adding *ly* to adjectives.

EXAMPLE: hopeful + ly = hopeful*ly*
ADJ.   ADV.

This kind of word-building helps you understand the way our language grows and also helps you learn to spell better when you come to double letters: local, loca*lly*; fearful, fearfu*lly*.

Write the correct form of noun, adjective, and adverb required in the spaces below. Use the endings *able, al, ible, ful, ly* as needed.

EXAMPLES:

hope + *ful* = hopeful + *ly* = hopefully
N.   ADJ.   ADV.

act + *al* = actual + *ly* = actually
N.   ADJ.   ADV.

force + *ible* = forcible + *ly* = forcibly
N.   ADJ.   ADV.

1 accident	accidental	_?_
2 incident	_?_	incidentally
3 _?_	natural	naturally
4 origin	_?_	originally
5 mechanic	_?_	_?_

123

6 fate	fatal	_?_
7 _?_	peaceful	_?_
8 occasion	_?_	occasionally
9 fear	fearful	_?_
10 love	lovable	_?_

E   Choose the correct meaning for each adverb below.

1   The captured thief gave up *meekly*.

(A) harshly   (B) roughly   (C) tamely

2   The judge spoke *mildly* to the witness.

(A) fiercely   (B) gently   (C) personally

3   The lawyer raised his voice *dramatically* before the jury.

(A) loudly   (B) foolishly   (C) theatrically

4   The courtroom listened *respectfully* to the verdict.

(A) excitedly   (B) quietly   (C) angrily

5   The defendant's mother sobbed *uncontrollably*.

(A) briefly   (B) endlessly   (C) unnecessarily

The more words you master, the richer become your thought processes.

PREPOSITIONS

WHAT'S MISSING FROM THESE SENTENCES?

Read these aloud.

The sun rises the morning and sets night.

Please go the bakery the corner fresh rolls.

I'd like one them butter right now.

The missing words are those little links that tie ideas together.

Read the same sentences with everything where it belongs.

The sun rises *in* the morning and sets *at* night.

Please go *to* the bakery *around* the corner *for* fresh rolls.

I'd like one *of* them *with* butter right now.

These connecting words are called ***prepositions***: *in, at, to, around, for, of, with*—and many more everyday words.

HOW ARE PREPOSITIONS USED IN A SENTENCE?

A preposition is the first word in a phrase.

in the morning	*at* night
to the bakery	*around* the corner
of them	*with* butter

A preposition is followed by a noun (N.) or pronoun (PRON.).

for the people
N.

after lunch
N.

by everybody
PRON.

to him
PRON.

near us
PRON.

across the street
N.

A preposition shows the relation between words in a sentence.

We shared a box *of* candy.
prep.

The train went *off* the track.
prep.

She ate lunch *with* me.
prep.

We found a piece *from* the puzzle.
prep.

Definition	A *preposition* is a word used to show how a noun or pronoun is related to another word in a sentence.

LIST OF PREPOSITIONS

at	by	to
into	for	from
of	off	about
down	during	near
up	with	between
among	on	over
under	below	behind
like	through	above
below	until	across
beyond	beside	except

126

Kick-off time / **COMPLETING SENTENCES WITH PREPOSITIONS**

Write the *prepositions* needed to complete these sentences.

1 I paid the money __?__ the man __?__ the door.

2 Lisa went __?__ Matthew __?__ the Disney Parade.

3 If you stand too __?__ the edge of the platform, you may fall __?__ the train.

4 When you climb __?__ a tree, hold tight or else you may fall __?__ the branch.

5 The Statue __?__ Liberty was made __?__ a French sculptor and came as a gift __?__ the French people.

Carry the ball / **PREPOSITIONS CHANGE THE MEANING**

By using different *prepositions*, you change the meaning of a group of words. Can you explain these statements? Act each one out to make clear what happens.

1		*on*
2		*over*
3		*under*
4		*across*
5	Tom threw the book	*near*	the desk.
6		*beside*
7		*behind*
8		*below*
9		*against*
10		*off*

You must take care in using words in order to say what you mean!

127

Prepositional Phrases

> **A** *prepositional phrase* **is a group of words beginning with a preposition and ending with a noun or pronoun.**

Here are some samples; the prepositional phrases are enclosed in parentheses.

Please sit *(in* the blue *chair.)*
        prep.   **noun**

(At the *store)* we met Tom.
prep. **noun**

The glass fell *(off* the *table.)*
        prep.   **noun**

The next number belongs *(to you.)*
        prep. pron.

Will you leave some cake *(for us?)*
        prep. pron.

Block that kick / **PREPOSITIONS INTRODUCE PREPOSITIONAL PHRASES**

Write each *prepositional phrase* on your answer paper and underline the *preposition* used to introduce the phrase.

1 Let's go for a short walk.

2 Of the two stories, I liked this one better.

3 I shall see you at home.

4 Alice received a letter from her brother.

5 In two minutes the game should start.

6 We hiked up the mountain.

7 Around the corner ran the frightened boy.

8   He looked about the house until he found his wallet.

9   You surely will not miss me; I'll stand near the bus stop.

10   We became good friends during the term.

Just a warm-up / **WRITE PHRASES**

Answer these questions by writing a *prepositional phrase.*

1   Where did you go on your vacation?

I went __?__ on my vacation.

2   How did you go there (by car, boat, or plane)?

I went there __?__.

3   Whom did you go with?

I went __?__.

4   When do you do your homework or study?

I do my homework or study __?__.

5   What time do you get up in the morning?

I usually get up __?__.

Pick up some extra yardage / **WRITE SENTENCES WITH PHRASES**

Write sentences using these *prepositional phrases.*

1   down the hill   4   for a good time

2   in a large house   5   beyond Ann's reach

3   on the top shelf

Just a pushover / **CHOOSING PREPOSITIONS TO FIT THE MEANING**

Write suitable *prepositions* to complete these sentences. Also, write the other preposition that appears in each sentence.

1 The quickest way to Europe is __?__ plane.

2 Cut the cake __?__ the sharp knife that we received from Uncle Joe.

3 In baseball, you hit the ball __?__ a bat.

4 We rode along the Parkway and left __?__ Exit 15.

5 Do you ever wonder what is __?__ the hill or under the sea?

Some Prepositions Have a Special Use and Meaning in a Sentence

Learn to use these prepositions the right way. Read the sentences aloud.

IN and *INTO*

He dived *in* the water.

(This means he was already standing in the water and jumped.)

He dived *into* the water.

(This means he was out of the water and then jumped into it.)

BETWEEN and *AMONG*

Divide this bag of cherries *between* Lisa and Matthew.

(For two persons, use "between.")

Divide this bag of cherries *among* Lisa, Matthew, and Monica.

(For three or more persons, use "among.")

FROM and *OFF*

Take the coat *from* Johnny.

(Johnny will hand it to you.)
(He may not be wearing it.)

Take the coat *off* Johnny.

(You will remove it or help him because he is wearing it.)

Point after touchdown / **PREPOSITIONS WITH A DIFFERENCE**

A   Explain the difference in meaning between each pair of sentences.

1   Larry walked *in* the cafeteria.

Larry walked *into* the cafeteria.

2   Share the popcorn *between* the two of us.

Share the popcorn *among* all of us.

3   He took the toy *from* his brother.

He took the toy *off* his brother.

B   Write original sentences using the above prepositions correctly.

1	*in*	*3*	*between*	*5*	*from*
2	*into*	*4*	*among*	*6*	*off*

Extra Prepositions Are Not Needed. Leave Them Out!

One too many!

I wonder where she is *at*.
I wonder where she is. (Omit *at*.)

He fell off *of* the chair.
He fell off the chair. (Omit *of*.)

In which bed will I sleep *in*?
In which bed will I sleep? (Omit *in*.)

To whom should I give this *to*?
To whom should I give this? (Omit *to*.)

For what is he crying for?
What is he crying for? (Omit *For*.)

Too many cooks . . . / **ONE TOO MANY**

Pick out the *extra* prepositions in the following sentences.

1   In which city were you born in?

2   For whom are you going to vote for?

3   Do you know in which house she is staying at?

4   Somebody pushed Tim off of the diving board.

5   To what store do you plan to go to?

6   I wonder about what new taxes he is thinking about.

7   This couch was designed for sitting, not sleeping on.

8   From whom are you going to borrow a pen from?

9   The Mayor is the leader under whom we taxpayers live under.

10   With whom did Ellen stop to talk with?

In This Lesson We Learned

A *preposition* is a word showing the relation between a noun or pronoun and another word in the sentence. Use prepositions according to their meaning to connect ideas.

To reach out to people, you must use words with their recognized meaning.

WORD-STUDY USING PREPOSITIONS

Prepositions are small words showing time, place, or manner when introducing a phrase. Notice these three kinds of phrases.

TIME	PLACE	MANNER
after lunch	under the table	with pleasure
between innings	over the treetop	in a hurry
for one year	along the river	by good luck
before bedtime	through the woods	without trying
during recess	on the radio	into a tizzy

EXERCISES

A   Using any of the *prepositional phrases* listed above, complete the following sentences.

1   Whenever we took a walk __?__, we avoided touching poison

ivy.

2   The announcement of the first prize in the cooking contest put

Laura Franks __?__.

3   We accept __?__ your kind invitation to come to the birthday

party.

4   Frankie and Johnny sold popcorn, candy, and peanuts at the

baseball game __?__.

5   Do you remember every night to say your prayers __?__?

B   Write five sentences using any of the prepositional phrases
listed previously.

C   Prepositions are used to show opposite action or change of
direction. For example:

>   PEDDLER: May I step *inside* the door?
>   HOUSEWIFE: No! Just stay *outside* the door!

You may add other prepositions to the list below: up/down,
etc.

OPPOSITE EXPRESSIONS

before/after	along/away from
above/below	through/around
in front of/behind	upon/beneath
near/far from	with/without
during/after	in/out
on/off	inside/outside

D   In place of each italicized preposition, write the opposite expression that fits the meaning in place of the one given.

1   When he lost his house key, he had to climb *out* the window.

2   On an envelope, you should paste the stamp *far from* the top right corner.

3   For safe driving, keep your car a hundred feet *in front of* the others.

4   Avoid getting fat because it's better to be *with* excess weight.

5   A submarine rides more easily *upon* the water.

E   Write five sentences using any of the prepositions given in the list in *C*. Then write the opposite expressions.

Choose your prepositions as neatly as a painter chooses his colors.

CONJUNCTIONS

Read these groups of words aloud. Which is the connecting word?

(a)   Sugar *and* spice.
(b)   Of the people *and* for the people.
(c)   We love our country, *and* we pledge allegiance to the flag.

We call *and* a **conjunction** because it connects words, phrases, and clauses.

words   in *(a)*   sugar + spice
phrases in *(b)*   of the people + for the people
clauses in *(c)*   we love our country + we pledge allegiance
                       to the flag

Besides *and*, we use as conjunctions *but, or.*

> Conjunctions (*and / or / but*) are used to connect words, phrases, and clauses. They show connections between ideas.

When used between two long clauses, place a comma before *and/or/but*. For short clauses, no comma is needed. Examples:

Tom looks handsome **and** Johnny looks untidy.

We have given billions, but we have not gained true friends.

                    comma

Conjunctions connect ideas in three different ways to show different meanings.

137

MEMORIZE THIS CHART

and	means something else is *added*
or	means there is another *choice* or other way
but	means an opposite or *contrast* is given

EXAMPLES

a. Mother tends to the house and children,
and Father earns the money for expenses.

(Mother tends + Father earns) → **added idea**

b. You may travel to Spain by jet plane,
or you may take the longer trip by boat.

(plane *or* boat) → **choice or other way**

c. Dieting may be good for some persons,
but exercise is good for everybody.

(dieting *but* exercise) → **contrast shown**

Quick quiz / **WRITING CONJUNCTIONS**

Write the suitable *conjunctions* that fit these sentences. Remember to choose the ones required by the meaning!

1 First she took lessons in scuba diving, __?__ then she got a certificate for lifesaving.

2 I never used to eat cucumbers, __?__ now I am getting to like them in mixed salads.

3 "Give me my deposit __?__ I'll take you to court," said the tenant.

4 Save some money for a rainy day, __?__ you may be sorry!

5 Many teen-agers flew to Europe last summer, __?__ the airlines refused to fly them back until they paid extra.

Word-Pairs

Some common word-pairs use conjunctions to tie them together. You have probably seen or heard these couples.

sweet *or* sour   hot *or* cold
tired *but* happy   hurt *but* silent
young *and* gay   willing *and* able

Get the idea? / **CONJUNCTIONS CONNECT
PAIRS OF WORDS**

Write the conjunctions *(and/or/but)* that fit these *word-pairs.*

1 She lost the trophy, a bit angry —?— smiling.

2 We decided to go fishing, rain —?— shine.

3 Bob practices golf all the time, summer —?— winter.

4 My wallet is gone, either lost —?— stolen.

5 To succeed in your ambition, you need not only pluck —?— luck.

Try another / **CONJUNCTIONS CONNECT
PAIRS OF PHRASES**

The same way as word-pairs, you find *two phrases in a row,* connected by *and/or/but.*

EXAMPLE: not in the evening *but* in the morning

Write the conjunctions needed to connect these phrases.

1 One duty of a secretary is opening the mail —?— sorting it out.

2 Don't sign your name under the line __?__ over it.

3 Dust some powder on your toes after bathing __?__ not before bathing.

4 Gold miners found gold either in the mountains __?__ in the rivers.

5 Hordes of adventurers dug into the hills __?__ sifted the streams.

Tie them together neatly / **USING CONJUNCTIONS**

In each statement below, write the correct choice of conjunction or connecting word *(and/or/but)*.

1 They leveled the slope with a bulldozer, __?__ later on they put wire baskets filled with stone to hold the earth.

2 The gas engine made quite a racket, __?__ the man running it did not seem to mind it.

3 The court ordered him to appear for a hearing, __?__ the judge would issue a warrant for his arrest.

4 He wanted to avoid putting in a new retaining wall, __?__ the regulations required him to build it.

5 He sold the property at a profit, __?__ he bought another house in a new development.

The name of the game / **WRITING SENTENCES**

Write original sentences using *and* / *or* / *but*. Two for each.

> **In This Lesson We Learned**
>
> *Conjunctions* connect words, phrases, and clauses. Different relationships between ideas are expressed by *and* / *or* / *but*.

INTERJECTIONS

You're blind!

An *interjection* is any word or phrase used to show your personal reaction, especially if it is something sudden, unexpected, and surprising. It may be good or bad, pleasant or unpleasant, happy or sad.

When you accidentally catch your finger in a door, do you say, "Ouch!" or "Ow!" or some other strong word to show sudden feelings? If you are surprised by a birthday party, do you say, "Hurrah!" or "Oh, my gosh!" or whatever you think will let out your emotion? These expressions that show sudden feelings are called *interjections*.

LIST OF INTERJECTIONS

Can you add any others?

Oh!	You bet!	Hello!
Ah!	Never!	Great!
Alas!	Not on your life!	Beautiful!
Well!	By gosh!	Hail to the chief!
Hurrah!	Forget it!	Oh shucks!
All right!	So sorry!	Nonsense!

Use your imagination / **WRITE INTERJECTIONS THAT SHOW STRONG FEELINGS**

Write an *interjection* to fit the sense or mood shown in each of these statements.

EXAMPLE: I'm glad you're here.   *Welcome!*

1   You just missed the train by two minutes.

2   Why should I lend you money again?

3   Be quiet so that we can hear the actors.

4   I'm so glad you won first prize in the race.

5   Don't touch the third rail; it will kill you!

Let yourself go! / **WRITE SENTENCES USING INTERJECTIONS**

Write sentences that are suggested by these *interjections*.

1   What a life!   4   Nonsense!

2   At last!   5   Beware!

3   Three cheers!

142

A FEW POINTS TO REMEMBER ABOUT INTERJECTIONS

- They are usually found in everyday talk, but rarely in writing.
- They do not form part of the sentence. They stand apart as a kind of outburst of feeling.
- They are usually punctuated with an exclamation point (!) to show that they are sudden expressions of feeling.
- They are very important in signs posted as warning of danger.

Here are a few examples:

on medicine bottles:	CAUTION! KEEP OUT OF REACH OF CHILDREN!
on road signs:	SLOW! ACCIDENT AHEAD!
on paint cans:	CAUTION! DO NOT INHALE FUMES!
on cleaners:	POISON! DO NOT SWALLOW!

FOR EXTRA CREDIT

Copy samples of interjections from your own observation at home, in school, and elsewhere.

In This Lesson We Learned

Interjections are words used to show sudden feelings; such as, shock, surprise, danger, etc.

REVIEWING THE EIGHT PARTS OF SPEECH

Use this as a handy reference whenever you want to refresh your memory.

noun: a word used as the name of a person, place, or thing.
Disney, California, boat

pronoun: a word used instead of a noun.
he, that, it

verb: a word used to show action or state of being.
go, sell, is

adjective: a word used to describe a noun.
red, old, fancy

adverb: a word used to modify a verb, an adjective, or another adverb.
hastily, very, surely

preposition: a word used to introduce a phrase.
to, in, at

conjunction: a word used to connect words, phrases, clauses.
and, or, but

interjection: a word used to show sudden feelings.
Ouch! Help! Hurrah!

144

> *A brief review of fundamentals will help you build more effective sentences.*

EXERCISES

A   The "parts of speech" are the way we can tell how words are *used* in a sentence. For each italicized expression, write its part of speech, using the following abbreviations. When in doubt, review the definitions on the previous page.

N.	=	noun	**ADV.**	=	adverb
PRON.	=	pronoun	**PREP.**	=	preposition
V.	=	verb	**CONJ.**	=	conjunction
ADJ.	=	adjective	**INTERJ.**	=	interjection

1   Girls like to go to a pajama *party.*

2   Boys would rather play baseball *or* other sports.

3   Our class *invited* the school nurse to talk about health.

4   Another day the friendly policeman spoke *about* safety.

5   We went home feeling good after a *perfect* day.

6   Everybody told *his* pals what a great game we played.

7   *"Happy landing!"* we shouted as the jet liner roared away.

8   *Sometimes* I can't even remember my own telephone number.

B   The same word may be used either as a *noun* or a *verb* in a sentence. Always look to see how the word is used before you decide on its part of speech. Label the italicized words *N* or *V*.

EXAMPLE: The *fly* could not *fly* away from the sticky paper.
           N.   V.

1   Tom tried to *head* for the door but bumped his *head*.

2   Barbara *dances* one of the latest *dances* in the talent show.

3   Matthew *drinks* fruit juices, especially orange *drinks*.

4   The blue *paint* was just the right color to *paint* the sky.

5   I did not hear the *yell* when my sister *yelled* for help.

C   For each italicized word, write the part of speech according to the way it is used in the sentence. Remember to figure out the actual use; not to guess!

1   *A*   How much time a day do you spend watching *television*?

      B   Which is your favorite *television* program?

2   *A*   *Orange* is my favorite fruit.

      B   For breakfast I always have *orange* juice.

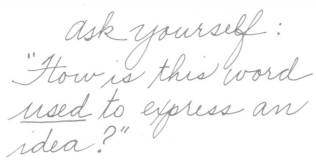
ask yourself:
"How is this word used to express an idea?"

3   A   Let's *clean* the car together.

     B   Father likes a *clean* car.

4   A   Please *tie* the package securely.

     B   I bought a new *tie* to match my blue suit.

5   A   Do this for no one else *but* me.

     B   I started to walk quickly, *but* I arrived late anyway.

6   A   I *like* sour cream on a baked potato.

     B   It looks just *like* whipped cream.

7   A   Ann *looks* so neat and tidy.

     B   Some of the boys admire *looks* more than personality.

8   A   He came toward the *opened* door.

     B   He smiled as the door *opened*.

9 *A* Driving at high *speed* may cause an accident.

   B When he sits at the wheel, he becomes a *speed* demon.

10 *A* At the right price, we will *buy* it.

   B When the price is right, it will be a good *buy*.

REVIEWING ERRORS IN USAGE

Your writing as well as that of other pupils reveals certain basic errors. With study and practice you can learn to avoid mistakes. Carefully select the correct expressions in the tests that follow.

```
┌─────────────────────────────┐
│          PLEASE!            │
│   Don't write in this book. │
│   Use separate sheets.      │
└─────────────────────────────┘
```

TEST I

Write the correct choice in each sentence.

1 I should have (stood, stayed) home yesterday.

2 They must have (did, done) it for fun.

3 Where (was, were) you this morning?

4   We were so thirsty we (drank, drunk) all the water.

5   There (are, is) five players on a basketball team.

6   Too bad they have (went, gone) away already.

7   He (couldn't, could) hardly read the daily newspaper.

8   Please hand me (them, those) books over there.

9   At last the passing bell (rang, rung) for recess.

10   (Him and me, He and I) are going to the game together.

11   Gale can sing pretty (good, well) as soprano.

12   He (don't, doesn't) know the way to do it.

13   I'm sure I (seen, saw) her on the bus.

14   This kind of fur coat looks (much, more) nicer.

15   Mike didn't have (any, no) film in his camera.

16   The coach (taught, learned) us how to throw a pass.

17   He must (of, have) gone to the field house.

18   (Who's, Whose) sneakers are in my locker?

19   They put them in (themselves, theirselves), I think.

20   I (brang, brought) the chess set to play after school.

21   The Yanks (won, won from) the Mets two games in a row.

22   (This, This here) desk was cleaned and polished like new.

23   It (ain't, isn't) raining anymore now, is it?

24   I'll bet that football is (ours, our's) from the last game.

25   Why don't you let (us, we) fellows pay for the pizza?

TEST II

Write the correct form of the word given in parentheses.

1   With a little luck our team could have (**beat**) them.

2   You should have (**go**) with us on the bus.

3   Neither my brother nor I (**be**) able to play the accordion.

4   I (**learn**) piano and guitar before the violin.

5   Mary and her friends (**be**) going ice-skating in the park.

6   The messenger (**bring**) the package to the front door.

7   At the close of school, the dismissal bell (**ring**) out.

8   If you don't try to be polite, you may become even (**rude**).

9   She looks taller and (**graceful**) than her cousin Susan.

10   When he asked for a vote, everybody raised (**his, their**) hand high.

TEST III

Write the correct spelling for the *plural* of each italicized noun in the following sentences.

1   I need a new pair of *shoe* three *time* during the year.

2   We put the *dish* in the washing machine and used the right *quantity* of soap powder and water.

3   Some *business* run special sales of rings and *wristwatch* after the holidays.

151

4 A group of young *thief* broke into some of our local *church* to rob the poor boxes last night.

5 Our school *secretary* decorated the office windows and *shelf* with colorful greeting cards.

6 If you had three *wish*, what special *request* would you make?

7 Yesterday we took her to the *laboratory* for some *X-ray* to find out what was wrong.

8 The ships in the *convoy* carrying supplies made several *journey* in the Atlantic and Pacific Oceans.

9 The leading *soprano* prefer to sing their *solo* with musical accompaniment.

10 The stories based on the *life* of great *hero* make fascinating reading for youngsters.

TEST IV

Write the correct spelling for the *possessive* of each italicized *pronoun* and *noun* in these sentences.

1 There was a *children* museum with an exhibit of spinning circles to catch *they* attention.

2 Because of the *referee* decision, the captain of our team lost *he* temper and got a warning.

3 At Christmas, we usually have a get-together of all members of *we* family at *Mother* house.

4 The *cowboys* roping contest ended with *they* lassoing a wild bronco.

5 Some *people* desire to own property leads them to invest their *life* savings in real estate.

6 *We* neighbors helped when a storm knocked down an old willow tree against *you* house.

7 City *officials* attendance honored the *rookie* funeral.

8 The *movie* title did not appeal to *him* imagination.

9 A *man* or *woman* value may not be measured by *others* opinions, but by his or her services to society.

10 *We* government guarantees *everyone* rights.

TEST V

Choose the correct *adjective* or *adverb* and write it on your answer paper. Remember that an adjective tells you *what kind;* an adverb answers the questions *how? when? where?*

1 After the snow melted, the streets became (**real, quite**) slushy for traffic.

2 When you paint bookshelves, apply the first coat (**thin, thinly**) to close the pores in the wood.

3 She spoke **(directly, direct)** to the class without turning her eyes left or right.

4 I wonder how **(happy, happily)** people could live if we all went back to the forest and caves.

5 The great size of modern cities makes us feel **(more lonely, more lonelier)** even when in a crowd.

6 The price of food and clothing always goes up **(more rapidly, more rapid)** than salaries.

7 A cold or cough makes you feel **(miserable, miserably)**.

8 If you take an aspirin about every three hours, you may get **(better, badder)** so long as you keep warm.

9 Remind him to sign his name **(neat and careful, neatly and carefully)** when he hands in his homework.

10 Our teacher marks our test papers **(fair and generous, fairly and generously)** to give us all a "break."

TEST VI

Sentence structure is based on grouping words to make sense.

INC = **incomplete sentence** — no subject/no verb/ not a complete thought

SF = **sentence fragment** — a phrase or a subordinate clause/not a sentence

S = **sentence** — complete thought with a subject and a verb

Read the sentences carefully and identify each as **INC, SF** or **S.**

1 Orange juice, milk, and eggs on toast for breakfast every morning.

2 Where the boys go fishing in the pond at the bottom of the hill.

3 In the near future, the television picture will be shown on your living room wall.

4 A contest between an American and a Russian for the chess championship of the world.

5 Our swimmers won many gold medals during the Olympic games.

6 She gave her father a small leather flask used for drinking wine in Spain.

7 Working two days a week instead of five days and taking things easy from now on.

8 The chief needs in the world today are peace, jobs, food, and shelter for all the people.

9 Wherever there exists slavery or injustice and human beings in tin shacks or straw huts.

10 The coaches gave the principal a beautiful plaque for expanding the sports program.

TEST VII

Can you tell whether the verb should be singular or plural? Write the word in parentheses that shows the correct *agreement between the subject and verb* in each sentence. Be very careful to notice when something comes between the subject and verb.

1 The leader of the troops (wears, wear) three stars on his cap.

2 Three aces (is, are) better than two pairs in a card game.

3 A work of art in three dimensions of wood or stone or steel (are, is) more natural looking.

4 John with his wife and children (looks, look) a bit crowded in that station wagon.

5 The road between the paved highways (consist, consists) of gravel covered with black top or asphalt.

6 In Austria you will see a beautiful castle with gardens that (stands, stand) on a hill.

7 Eggplants, goat cheese, tomatoes, and olive oil (make, makes) a delicious dish in the islands of Greece.

8 Sometimes the pages in a new book (are, is) not trimmed or cut at the edge.

9 A short list showing his possessions (contains, contain) first and foremost the names of his children.

10 Why (don't, doesn't) the schedule of ball games print a little star to tell which ones are played at home?

TEST VIII

Select the right word to fit the meaning in each of the following sentences.

1 He came to school (around, about) ten minutes late.

2 When he walked (in, into) the building, he met some friends near the entrance.

3 Peter had some donuts which he offered to share (among, between) several pals.

4 In order to finish his homework, Tom borrowed a pen (off, from) his cousin Frank.

5 Everybody likes rock and roll (except, accept) the squares who prefer the oldtime songs.

6 Smoky the Bear was the animal (which, who) was chosen to help fight forest fires.

7 Louis played tennis with his roommate, (which, who) came from a college out West.

8 The astronauts drank orange juice prepared from TANG, (which, who) contains the natural vitamins.

9 Why don't you come (to, over) my house tomorrow to play a game of checkers?

10 Maureen said she will be sleeping (by, at) her girl friend's house after the party.

TEST IX

Capitalize only those words which are used as proper nouns (or proper adjectives) referring to specific places, persons, etc.

1   See the u.s.a. in a chevrolet.

2   Some neighbors collected funds for the red cross.

3   When the people's republic of china was admitted to the united nations, the nationalist government on the island of taiwan lost its seat.

4   Dan used to design ship propellers for the bethlehem steel corporation.

5   Traffic across the golden gate bridge was heavy on labor day.

6   The floodwaters of the mississippi river threatened every city from st. louis to new orleans.

7   Our local assemblyman jones serves on the state legislature.

8   The army corps of engineers is considering ways to check erosion of the beach.

9   We finally got the site for a replacement of lake drive high school.

10   The newspaper praised mayor connor for his efforts.

Just as there are rules for playing football or any other sport, there are rules for using language.

SENTENCE SKILL: MAKE PARTS PARALLEL

Whenever you put ideas into a sentence, try to keep the parts evenly balanced or parallel. Study these examples of parallel parts. Read them aloud.

LINE UP WORDS IN A ROW

1   She was fair, fat, and forty.
    (3 adjectives in a row)
2   Our Armed Services include soldiers, sailors, and marines.
    (3 nouns)
3   The lost youngster cried, shouted, and prayed for help.
    (3 verbs)

USE PHRASES IN SERIES

1   An Italian meal without wine is like a day without sunshine.
2   In youth we feel brave; in age we grow cautious.
3   Democracy is government of the people, by the people, and for the people.

159

MAKE CLAUSES THE SAME IN STRUCTURE

1 Tell me <u>who your friends are</u>, and I will tell you <u>who you are</u>.

2 The wheel <u>that squeaks</u> is the one <u>that gets the grease</u>.

3 <u>When you finish your chores</u> is the time <u>when you will get your allowance</u>.

AVOID AWKWARDNESS DUE TO LACK OF PARALLEL PARTS

a AWKWARD: He was tall, slim, and *had lots of muscle.*

   BETTER: He was tall, slim, and *muscular.*
      (**3 adjectives:** tall, slim, muscular)

b AWKWARD: Should we go in, wait outside, or *just start ringing the bell?*

   BETTER: Should we go in, wait outside, or *ring the bell?*
      (**3 verbs:** go, wait, ring)

c AWKWARD: There were men who gave orders, men who worked on the job, and *a lot of other hangers-on just watching.*

   BETTER: There were men who gave orders, men who worked on the job, and *men who just watched.*
      (**3 clauses:** who gave orders, who worked on the job, who just watched)

Note:

In *a*, it is better to use a single adjective "muscular" instead of the awkward group "had lots of muscle."

In *b*, it is better to use the verb "ring" instead of the awkward expression "just start ringing the bell."

In *c*, it is better to use the clause "who just watched" instead of the awkward "a lot of other hangers-on just watching."

Write this way! / **WRITE BETTER SENTENCES**

A Add some *words in a row* to these sentences.

1 The boss likes his new secretary because she is always prompt, courteous, __?__ and __?__. (adjectives)

2 The wastebasket contained all kinds of refuse: bottles, cans, __?__ and __?__. (nouns)

3 Whenever she heard a joke she used to giggle, laugh, __?__ and __?__. (verbs)

4 The horses dashed around the race track speedily, __?__ and __?__. (adverbs)

5 As she received the trophy, she looked very much surprised, __?__ and __?__. (adjectives)

B Write another *phrase* to keep the parts even or parallel in each of these sentences.

1 If you can't come in through the door, you'll have to try to come in __?__.

2 To dry your swimsuit, hang it on the clothesline or put it __?__.

3 When you tell a fish story to a group, tell it with words and dramatize __?__.

4 I think it is much harder driving at night than __?__.

5 I'd like to do something good for everybody but especially __?__.

C   Write another *clause* to balance each sentence below.

1   The kind of music that youngsters enjoy is quite different from the kind that ___?___.

2   I remember the house where I was born, but I have forgotten the place where ___?___.

3   Try these shoes which are your right size instead of trying those which ___?___.

4   "Pebbles" used to run when we threw a stick into the water and come back when ___?___.

5   That's the kind of person who makes frequent phone calls and who ___?___.

D   The italicized parts are out of step with the rest. Rewrite these sentences so that all parts are *parallel*.

1   She came home from shopping somewhat tired, sticky, and *feeling annoyed about it.*

2   The dessert turned out to be delicious, delightful, and *it tasted pretty good.*

3   If you earn money, save a little, spend a little, and *then maybe invest in something worthwhile*, you will be doing all right.

4   The ones who make the loudest noise are usually the ones who do the least work, yet *they are always ready to complain about everything.*

5   The men crushed the rocks, mixed them with dirt, and *put everything together with cement.*

In This Lesson We Learned

   To write better sentences, try to keep *words* in a row, *phrases* in pairs, *clauses* balanced so that these parts are even or parallel.

SENTENCE SKILL: AVOID WRONG POSITION OF WORDS

To make your meaning clear, you must put words together in the right order. If you put words in the wrong position, you miss the point of whatever you want to say. Sometimes the word in the wrong place may change the meaning or make the idea ridiculous. Be careful in sentences like those below!

Position Changes the Meaning

1 If I *only* had a dollar.   (I had nothing else; I wished I had a dollar.)

2 If *only* I had a dollar.   (If I were the single person with a dollar, then no one else would have any.)

3 If I had *only* a dollar.   (At least one dollar would be enough for me.)

4 Tom has *just* arrived.   (When did Tom get here? He just arrived now.)

5 *Just* Tom has arrived.   (Is everybody here? Not yet. Just Tom has arrived.)

6   He guessed *almost* all the answers.   ⌣↗   (He did not guess all, but almost all the answers.)

7   He *almost* guessed all the answers. ⌣↗   (He figured out some, and then he almost guessed the answers.)

For clear thinking / **PUT WORDS IN PROPER ORDER**

How does the position of the italicized word change the meaning in each pair of sentences?

1   We came here *only* to see you.

(Why did we come here?)

2   *Only* we came here to see you.

(Did anybody else come here?)

3   Dad planted *just* tomatoes this week.

(Did Dad plant anything else?)

4   Dad planted tomatoes *just* this week.

(How long ago did Dad plant them?)

5   The *last* man hired is the *first* one fired.

(What happens to the last man hired?)

6   The *first* man hired is the *last* one fired.

(Why does the man with longest service stay?)

7   I *too* want to see the manager.

(Does somebody else want to see him?)

8   I want to see the manager *too*.

(Besides the cashier and sales clerk, whom will I see?)

164

9   He was *about* through at three o'clock.

(When had he almost finished the job?)

10   He was through at *about* three o'clock.

(What time was it when he finished?)

"Danglers"

Sometimes a group of words "dangles" in the wrong place because it lacks a good sense connection with the rest of the sentence. Such danglers or misplaced parts may appear laughable because they are near the wrong word or just hang nowhere.

Read these samples aloud. *What's wrong?*

1   Talking to Mother, the cake burned in the oven.

(Who was talking to Mother?)

2   After cutting the lawn, the mower was put back into the garage.

(Who put the mower into the garage?)

3   The piano tuner tested the keyboard having nimble fingers.

(Who has nimble fingers?)

Here's the *right way!* Put things where they belong to make sense.

1   While Betty was talking to Mother, the cake burned in the oven.

2   After cutting the lawn, I put the mower back into the garage.

3   With nimble fingers, the piano tuner tested the keyboard.

165

Arrange words to convey the meaning you want to get across.

Apply first-aid / **AVOID "DANGLERS"**

Re-arrange these sentences to avoid "danglers." Put the loose part near the word where it belongs, or else add the words needed to make clear the meaning.

1 Walking downstairs, my foot tripped on a step.

2 Hurrying inside, the movie had just begun.

3 Welcoming the foreign visitors, champagne was served.

4 Being rather tired and sleepy, the party ended early.

5 Acting on a tip provided by another player, the horse paid eight to one at the betting window.

6 After finishing lunch and playing ball, the bell rang for going back to school.

7 He refused to sit in the barber's chair having such long hair.

8 The detectives found the jewels belonging to the actress lying in the gutter.

9 Having nothing better to do in the evening, the TV goes on for hours.

10 Cruising down the river, the lovely moon shone up in the sky.

In This Lesson We Learned

Sentence skill in avoiding the wrong position of words will help make the meaning clear. Avoid "danglers" by rearranging the sentence or adding some necessary words.

166

SENTENCE SKILL: USE A VARIETY OF PATTERNS

You have heard the saying, "Variety is the spice of life." How about a little variety in sentences, too? Always having the subject at the beginning gets a bit dull. Then, having the verb tag along makes sentences all the same. Nothing's wrong in having subject and verb in that order, but maybe it would be more lively if you could change things around. Say what you mean, but avoid repeating the way you put your ideas together.

Here are five ways for getting variety in your sentences. (**S** = subject, **V** = verb, **O** = object)

GETTING VARIETY

I   Begin with the object instead of the subject.

THE USUAL WAY: I like you.   I can't stand Oscar.
                  S. V.   O.   S.   O.
                                        \ V. /

FOR VARIETY: You I like.   Oscar I can't stand.
                  O. S. V.   O.   S.
                                              \ V. /

II   Start with the verb instead of the subject.

THE USUAL WAY: You may dress anyway you like for the
                  S.   V.
                  party.

FOR VARIETY: Dress anyway you like for the party.
                  V.

167

To obtain variety in your sentences, arrange some parts a little differently.

III Put an adverb first, or an adverb phrase.

THE USUAL WAY: He jumped to his feet suddenly.
ADV.

FOR VARIETY: Suddenly, he jumped to his feet.
ADV.

THE USUAL WAY: You will feel lonely without your friend.
phrase

FOR VARIETY: Without your friend, you will feel lonely.
phrase

IV Begin with an adjective or two.

THE USUAL WAY: The hikers, hungry and tired,
ADJ. **ADJ.**
could go no further.

FOR VARIETY: Hungry and tired, the hikers
ADJ. **ADJ.**
could go no further.

V Start with a clause instead of the main idea.

THE USUAL WAY: I began when he gave the signal.
clause

FOR VARIETY: When he gave the signal, I began.
clause

Take another look at the sample sentences given above as "THE USUAL WAY." You will notice that they all follow the order of subject and verb. That's all right, but tiresome. Now notice the five ways given as "FOR VARIETY." Just remember to start your sentences sometimes a bit differently by using first the object, or the verb, or an adverb, or an adjective, or a phrase, or a clause. You can do it if you try!

168

Following the five ways of getting variety in your sentences, re-write these sentences as directed.

A   Begin with the object instead of the subject.

1   We all need a friend.

2   Mike hit a home run.

3   The umpire shouted, "Safe!"

4   You can always use cash.

5   We called Mary first.

B   Start with the verb instead of the subject.

1   You ought to try to get a part-time job.

2   You may come right inside to see the manager.

3   The way to find gold is to dig.

4   You can catch a falling star in the desert.

5   With good friends you will enjoy traveling.

C   Put an adverb first, or an adverb phrase.

1   There's a smog hanging over the city.

2   The sunlight seems shut out by gray clouds.

3   City dwellers wish for rain, hopefully.

4 The game warden watches hunters suspiciously.

5 The restoration of the old mansion stood proudly.

   D *Begin with an adjective or two.*

1 The shoppers, young and old, rushed in for the sale.

2 You will like the flavor, natural and not artificial.

3 My sister, alone but unafraid, chased the snake away.

4 In a special tomb sleeps the soldier unknown by name.

5 A person who smiles and says "hello" is happy.

   E *Start with a clause instead of the main idea.*

1 This fat-free milk is good for those who are overweight.

2 One chubby boy said that grapefruit juice trimmed his figure.

3 Never try a reducing diet unless your doctor approves.

4 Take fruit, nuts, or cheese after you finish the main dish.

5 You still need some starches if you want to balance the proteins.

Here's how! / **WRITE BETTER SENTENCES**

Re-write these sentences using something else besides the subject to begin. Suggestions: a phrase, a clause, the verb, the object, etc.

1 The leader of the band walked briskly straight to the "mike."

2 I wonder what would happen if some nation panicked and fired a nuclear bomb by mistake.

3 We are going to work this thing out, all together.

Never again will your sentences fail because of the mechanical repetition or monotonous sameness of expression!

SAME STUFF SAME STUFF SAME STUFF

4 He scraped the slope, loaded trap-rock into wire baskets, and built a retaining wall, using inexperienced labor.

5 I found the book you were looking for where you wouldn't expect.

6 We sat on the front porch facing the moonrise every evening.

7 Listen to Louis as he plays that kind of "blues" and "pop rock."

8 I'm with you, whatever you may do.

9 Laura has only a thin dime in her purse after her trip.

10 You deserve this award for bravery under fire.

In This Lesson We Learned

For variety in sentences, you may begin with other things besides the usual subject. Try starting with the object, the verb, an adverb, an adjective, a phrase, or a clause.

SENTENCE SKILL: RE-WRITE RUN-ON SENTENCES

A sentence stops with a period. If you run one sentence right on to the next sentence with a comma standing between them, you have a "run-on" or comma blunder.

Run-on sentences are two sentences separated by a comma instead of a period. Divide them into separate sentences.

RUN-ON: The light turned green, all the cars moved.

(The comma is not the way to divide ideas.)

CORRECT: The light turned green. All the cars moved.

(The period is the way to divide complete thoughts.)

Sometimes you can avoid run-on sentences by using connecting words to make one strong sentence.

BETTER: *When* the light turned green, all the cars moved.

(The word *when* introduces a helping clause.)

BETTER: The light turned green *just as* all the cars moved.

(The words *just as* connect the helping clause.)

172

How to Correct Run-on Sentences

There are several ways of changing a run-on into a sentence.

⭐ Change the second main clause into a *participial phrase* (ending *-ing*).

RUN-ON: Rowena drove into our carport, she honked the horn for Mary.

BETTER: Rowena drove into our carport, *honking* the horn for Mary.

⭐ Connect the two run-on sentences with a *conjunction (and/ or/but)*.

RUN-ON: Paul got to school early, he got to class late somehow.

BETTER: Paul got to school early, *but* he got to class late somehow.

⭐ Change one of the two main clauses into a *subordinate clause* (using such connectives as *when, after, since, because,* etc.).

RUN-ON: She took an aspirin, her toothache still felt bad.

BETTER: *Although* she took an aspirin, her toothache still felt bad.

⭐ Change one of the main clauses into a *phrase* (adjective or adverb).

RUN-ON: Mark Spitz was a champion swimmer, he trained for the Olympics for many years and won seven gold medals.

BETTER: Mark Spitz, a champion swimmer, *trained* for the Olympics for many years and won seven gold medals.

⭐ Separate the two sentences by using a period instead of a comma.

RUN-ON: The race was over, the crowd left the field.

BETTER: The race was over. The crowd left the field.

Use a *semicolon* between the two main clauses if close in meaning.

RUN-ON: The doctor tried everything, in the end he saved the boy.

BETTER: The doctor tried everything; in the end he saved the boy.

Don't make this mistake / **PUT AN END TO RUN-ONS**

Re-write these *run-on sentences* by using some of the suggested ways explained previously.

1 She took the return flight from Miami, it arrived in Newark in two hours.

2 She found her baggage, she looked around for her friend.

3 The airport was crowded with passengers, she called for a porter.

4 He carried the bags to the curb, her father came to meet her.

5 They looked suntanned and happy, he seemed tired and hungry.

6 She rented a bike to go to the beach, her grandmother prepared supper for her.

7 All day she basked in the sun, the weather in Florida was fair and mild.

8 Occasionally, she took a dip in the ocean, the water looked green and cool.

9 Everybody seemed to take it easy down South, what a wonderful winter vacation that was.

10 Next day she went back to school, the memory of the trip lingered on.

Five of these are correct sentences. Label them *CS*. The other fifteen are run-on sentences. Correct them by dividing them into two separate sentences, or make them single sentences by adding a connecting word.

1   The invention of the printing press made books available to more people.

2   A mountain slide brought tons of snow, it buried a village.

3   Nearby folk helped the victims of the plane crash, the nearby church served as an emergency hospital.

4   Such disasters occur in the ski areas of France and Switzerland because of the high altitudes.

5   Sports lovers dare the highest slopes, they seek adventure and excitement.

6   An ancient aqueduct brings water down to Rome, it was built in the surrounding hills hundreds of years ago.

7   The stone bridges still stand, they serve today as safely as in days gone by.

8   Irrigation has changed deserts, the dry places have bloomed again.

9   Terracing or building steps in the hills, the Chinese have held back the soil against wind and rain.

10   Years ago our Western plains became "dust bowls," we cut down the trees and allowed cattle to overgraze.

11   Plastic containers cause pollution, they do not dissolve like other waste materials.

12   Some of our rivers have been spoiled, the fish from these streams are not fit to eat.

13 Smog floats heavily over our big cities, who can breathe this air and live?

14 Supermarkets offer many bargains, their specials attract customers.

15 Wait a minute, please, I'm next in line to check out.

16 The manager signs the check before it can be cashed.

17 Is this your shopping cart, sir, why don't you put it back where it belongs?

18 A little courtesy makes life smoother, bad manners lose friends.

19 Vincent came over to ask for a baby-sitter in order that he might take Gale to see a movie.

20 Louis said he would help, he had finished all his homework.

No fumbling allowed / **WRITE CORRECT AND EFFECTIVE SENTENCES**

Complete these statements.

1 She and her friend rode their bikes to ...

2 Some car drivers came so close that ...

3 Next to the roadway was a sandy lane which ...

4 Suddenly, a little puppy chased alongside ...

5 Too much pedaling made their legs tired but ...

6 An artist makes a pencil sketch and ...

7 A camera takes a picture with ...

8   When you look at distant objects, they appear smaller because...

9   As a change in style, try to design with paper cut-outs ...

10 I like those original drawings that show imagination and avoid...

Story / **TELEVISION**

Re-write the following selection, replacing the blanks with words that make sense.

Do you like to listen to_____or_____on television? Some of the shows are_____and_____to watch. Even some of the top-notch comedy stars that_____becoming boring after_____. If you finish your school work, you may see some good movies _____. Around ten o'clock, the daily news broadcasts_____and weather reports. What my father likes to see are sports_____ mysteries_____detective stories. My mother prefers to watch "talk shows" like_____and "family problems" like_____. I guess we need more television sets in the house if_____and keep _____.

In This Lesson We Learned

A **run-on** sentence or **comma blunder** is two main ideas separated by a comma instead of a period. To avoid this,

• divide the run-on into two separate sentences,

• or make one strong sentence by using some connecting words and correct punctuation.

REVIEW TESTS IN SENTENCE SKILLS

TEST I   MAKING BETTER SENTENCES

You can improve your sentence structure by several methods:

Making ideas *parallel* by using words in a row, or phrases in a series, and clauses evenly balanced.

Avoiding the wrong *position* of words that dangle out of place without any connection to the sense.

Making a variety of *patterns* to express ideas; such as, *-ing* words (skating, etc.) in place of clauses, or starting the sentence with a phrase.

Using the *3 P's (parallel, position, patterns)*, re-write these sentences.

1   Youngsters like skating, hiking, and to ride a bicycle.

2   Sewers may become clogged with leaves, candy wrappers, soda cans, and careless droppings of rubbish.

3 The scout troop promised to obey the patrol leader, stay on the trail, notice the birds and trees, and nobody would get lost.

4 Buzzing around the pier, I saw a sea gull snatch a fish.

5 She found her earring opening her pocketbook.

6 While entering the Prado Museum in Madrid, the names of famous Spanish painters over the main entrance are seen.

7 With all the hullaballoo and baby-kissing, some of our politicians lose elections because they make empty promises, appeal to certain groups, and their record is poor.

8 God help you if I ever lay my hands on you in anger.

9 You may speak whenever I call your name just to keep the meeting orderly and give everyone a chance.

10 While parked in front of the house, some rascal scribbled "Please wash me" on the trunk of my car.

TEST II   POSITION CHANGES MEANING

Position of words changes the message. Can you explain the difference between each pair of sentences?

1 A Somebody was knocking on the hard door.

   B Somebody was knocking on the door hard.

2 A Have you ever seen a boat house?

   B Have you ever seen a house boat?

3 A I just want milk and crackers.

   B Just I want milk and crackers.

4 A We caught only blue fish yesterday.

   B Only we caught blue fish yesterday.

5   *A*   Mother spoke with the principal too.

     B   Mother too spoke with the principal.

TEST III   AVOIDING RUN-ON SENTENCES

Re-write these sentences correctly. Remember there are two ways of avoiding run-on sentences: (1) by dividing the two main ideas into separate sentences; or (2) by adding a connecting word between the two main ideas.

1   There she goes, just look at the way she skims across the ice with her fancy skates.

2   Look at those birds, they fly south across the sky in a perfect V-formation.

3   Let's go to the hamburger haven, I feel hungry enough to have a couple.

4   He sits quietly while in class, you should hear him outside in the playground.

5   The dentist tells you to brush your teeth regularly, the reason is that food particles cause decay.

6   Color television sets are still quite expensive to buy, some stories look just as good in black and white TV.

7   We tried to catch the early bus, we missed the one that carries all our friends.

8   Collecting scrap for re-use cleans the neighborhood, it also makes our natural resources last longer.

9   The young will always seek adventure, the old usually like peace and quiet at home.

10   Men have shuttled back and forth from the moon, the next big step will be to try to land on Mars.

TEST IV MAKING ONE STRONG SENTENCE OUT OF TWO

Combine two sentences into one strong sentence by connecting one idea to the other. To show this connection, use one of these words to fit the meaning:

because	where	after	before
since	although	as	who
when	if	until	but
while	unless	how	why

1 The players on both teams appeared strained. The coaches gave the signal to continue the game.

2 She put the pancakes on the griddle. She put the syrup on the table.

3 Tom made some poached eggs. He knew I liked them better than scrambled.

4 We will get permission to go on a trip. We must behave during the whole week.

5 Angelo is our regular postman. He delivers the mail with a smile.

6 Our old car still runs in good weather. The car battery is a bit weak for freezing mornings.

7 A short basketball player does not stand a chance against a tall player. They jump for the ball together.

8 The carpenter built the frame for the new house. The mason came to lay the bricks around the frame.

9 Please cover your books. They will be damaged by the rain.

10 Stand up and speak up. We want to see and hear you.

PUNCTUATION MARKS: END OF SENTENCE

The meaning of a group of words may change according to the punctuation marks at the end of a sentence. Read these sentences aloud.

"This is all mine now."   =   plain statement of fact
"This is all mine now?"   =   question raises a doubt
"This is all mine now!"   =   strong claim shown without doubt

"Please take one."   =   You may have one, with permission.
"Please take one?"   =   How many may you have?
"Please take one!"   =   You must have one and only one!

There are *three kinds of punctuation marks* used at the end of a sentence, depending on the meaning you want.

◇ **PERIOD**   **After a simple statement of fact.**

The bells are ringing.
Tomorrow we will have a holiday.

◇ **QUESTION**   **After a question or something in doubt.**

Are the bells ringing?
Will we have a holiday tomorrow?

◇ **EXCLAMATION**   **After a strong expression of feeling (fear, gladness, etc.).**

The bells are ringing!
Tomorrow we will have a holiday!

182

Get the point / **END PUNCTUATION—I**

Write the end punctuation mark for each of these sentences.

1   Do you still chew bubble gum

2   Shame on you

3   You ought to ask your dentist

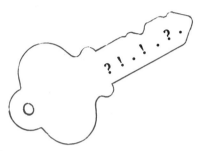

4   What a storm

5   She is going by plane

6   Has he ever swum this distance

7   Please direct me to the library

No through traffic / **END PUNCTUATION—II**

Write the proper punctuation marks at the end of these sentences.

1   Do we need more judges to enforce the laws,

or fewer laws to enforce

2   Did you purchase your new radio at a discount

*Each sentence must be solidly built
so that it states something clearly, asks
a question, gives a command, or
expresses strong feeling.*

3   Is your skin smooth and soft, or dry and flaky

4   The ending of the movie left me feeling sad

5   We use a timer to turn lights on at night

6   If you have any honest opinions, we'll listen

7   Don't let that rascal get away

8   The youngsters shouted, "Up with people "

9   The Mets are struggling for third place now

10 Cleaner exhausts in automobiles mean less pollution

Stop! Look before crossing / **END PUNCTUATION—III**

Change the *statements* to questions. Answer the *questions*.

1   At the equator, the natives wear few articles of clothing.

2   Water and sunshine and soil make tomatoes grow.

3   Can a thoroughbred run faster than a lion?

4   Which game do you like to play, baseball or football?

5   After a ball game we usually take a shower.

6   The street lights go on just before dark.

7   How can bank tellers recognize phony money?

8   Why do people move from the cities to the suburbs?

9   Wrestlers look like strong men trying to act rough.

10 Mother likes to keep porcelain figurines on the mantel.

Go when safe / **END PUNCTUATION—IV**

FROM THE NEWS

Supply the end punctuation for these sentences taken from the news. Remember the reason for using each mark (period, question, exclamation)!

1   Pollsters are asking people the wrong questions

2   Who will quarterback the team this Saturday

3   The bombs are falling everywhere, and civilians are getting killed

4   She liked the concert but added, "My goodness, it was loud "

5   Which of these cities provides the most police protection

6   When you put up a wall, whom are you really shutting out

7   Talcum powder with asbestos can lead to lung cancer

8   How will man get energy when the world runs out of gas and oil

9   You can feel and see summer wherever you are in Bermuda

10 Hey, you aren't going to win any gold medals

In This Lesson We Learned

There are **3** punctuation marks used to *end* a sentence:

- *period* for a statement of fact;
- *question* for something in doubt;
- *exclamation* for strong feeling.

PUNCTUATION MARKS: INSIDE A SENTENCE

Can you make any _sense_ out of these groups of words?

(1)

A boy or girl who will listen to the coach take notes and ask questions is a youngster who wants to learn I don't think they are interested in making the team if they never ask questions watch the clock and leave practice

(2)

All across the land citizens young and old are conscious of what's happening to our environment they are investigating complaints about pollution organizing tours to inspect offenders in the area starting programs for re-using materials and earning money by collecting empty bottles cans etc.

Punctuation makes the *meaning* clear! Read them this way.

A boy or girl who will listen to the coach, take notes, and ask questions is a youngster who wants to learn.* I don't think they are interested in making the team if they never ask questions, watch the clock, and leave practice.

*Instead of a period, a *semicolon* may be used here.

All across the land, citizens young and old are conscious of what's happening to our environment;* they are investigating complaints about pollution, organizing tours to inspect offenders in the area, starting programs for re-using materials, and earning money by collecting empty bottles, cans, etc.

*Instead of a semicolon, a *period* may be used here, and a capital *T* for *They*.

Punctuation *inside* a sentence includes these *three* marks:

| COMMA | SEMICOLON | COLON |

Here are some sample sentences showing the use of each kind of punctuation. Then we will take each one more fully.

The Right Way to Punctuate Inside a Sentence

1   She wore jewelry like earrings, bracelets, brooches, and necklaces.

    Commas separate a series of *words*.

2   Which is your favorite sport: basketball, baseball, or football?

    Colon introduces a series of words set off by *commas*.

The comma before *and/or* in the last of a series is optional.

187

3 Youngsters threaten to leave home; however, only a small number actually do.

> *Semicolon* separates main clauses using a *conjunction.*

4 I'll have orange juice and cereal with milk; I guess that's all today.

> *Semicolon* separates main clauses close in meaning.

Slow! Dangerous curve ahead / **INSIDE PUNCTUATION—I**

Write these sentences on your answer sheet, punctuating them correctly.

1 When the tiger finished eating the trainer cracked his whip.

2 What is your girl friend's name Mary Ann?

3 Banks sell coins in rolls pennies nickels dimes and quarters.

4 We tried the single-wing formation we scored on the next play.

5 We used every trick to keep the baby quiet but we had no success.

ANSWERS WITH EXPLANATIONS

1 When the tiger finished eating, the trainer cracked his whip.

> *Comma* separates the introductory clause "When the tiger finished eating" from the main clause. Otherwise, the tiger would eat the trainer!

2 What is your girl friend's name, Mary Ann?

> *Comma* shows that Mary Ann is the person spoken to.

3 Banks sell coins in rolls: pennies, nickels, dimes, and quarters.

> *Colon* introduces a series of things after the word *rolls.* *Commas* separate the items listed in a series.

4 We tried the single-wing formation; we scored on the next play.

> *Semicolon* separates the two main clauses, just as a period would (followed by a capital *W* for *We*). Since these clauses stand close in meaning, the semicolon is preferred.

5 We used every trick to keep the baby quiet, but we had no success.

> *Comma* before *but*.

Resume speed / **INSIDE PUNCTUATION—II**

Re-write these sentences and punctuate to make the meaning clear.

1 Well what are you going to do now?

2 Let's visit Frank he's got a boat a bike and a pool.

3 Yesterday he served spaghetti meat balls and tomato sauce.

4 He must be rich he has everything he wants.

5 I pity him he's got nothing else to aim for.

6 Vincent caught nine blues twelve porgies and three bass.

7 He cleaned them put some in the freezer and gave his friends the rest.

8 Invite him to your house no fuss just a little get-together.

9 Call him now why wait till you miss him?

10 Just as Margaret started typing her friend came to the door and invited her to go bowling.

> **In This Lesson We Learned**
>
> Punctuation *inside* a sentence makes the meaning clear. Use the comma, the semicolon, and the colon to separate ideas.

PUNCTUATION MARKS: USING THE COMMA

The most often used punctuation mark inside a sentence is the *comma*. **It is a signal to the reader to separate words and ideas.** Sometimes a missing comma makes a sentence seem awkward or nonsensical.

PUZZLES	Try reading these with no comma.
As he was putting the roof on his mother prepared lunch. While they were fishing on the fire all the pancakes burned. The day being young the old man slept.	

ANSWERS	A comma makes the meaning clear.
As he was putting the roof on, his mother prepared lunch. While they were fishing, on the fire all the pancakes burned. The day being young, the old man slept.	

Notice the difference in *meaning according to the position of the comma* in these sentences.

a. This is Tom's Father.   (Whose parent is this?)

This is Tom's, Father.   (Tell Dad to whom it belongs.)

b. Mary Ann, Betty Lou, and Frank sat in the boat.   (3 persons)

Mary Ann, Betty, Lou, and Frank sat in the boat.   (4 persons)

Mary, Ann, Betty, Lou, and Frank sat in the boat.   (5 persons)

c. My brother Peter and Lee visited us yesterday.   (2 persons)

My brother, Peter, and Lee visited us yesterday.   (3 persons)

RULES

When should you use the COMMA? Learn these rules!

To separate words in a series.

I like apples, peaches, pears, and bananas.

To separate a long clause at the beginning of a sentence.

When I think of all the good things our parents do to help, I wonder why we forget so quickly.

To separate main clauses connected by *and/or/but*.

He really wanted to apologize for being rude, *but* he never got a chance to say he was sorry.

Punctuation directs the reader's attention as surely as road signs lead the driver along a highway.

⌃_, To separate dates and places.

Lincoln was born on February 12, 1809.
We landed at Orly Airport near Paris, France.

⌃_, To set off the opening and the closing of a letter.

Dear Frank,

    I hope you are feeling better. We want you back on the team soon.

                            Your pal,
                            Tony

Commas are signals / **MAKE SENSE WITH COMMAS**

Re-write and punctuate correctly.

1   If all the people become aware of the dangers of air pollution steps will be taken to clean the air.

2   First she said she wanted to go shopping for a new coat and all of a sudden she said she preferred to go skating.

3   Dear Aunt Martha

    Please come to my birthday party November first.

                        Affectionately yours
                        Mary Ann

4   The World Trade Center is located in downtown Manhattan New York City.

5   Take whichever you like best: green blue yellow or gold.

6   According to official records Shakespeare's birthday came on April 23 1564.

7   Some banks pay different rates of interest depending on the amount deposited the time the money stays in the bank and the kind of account.

8   The A's won two in Cincinnati one at Oakland; at last they won number four in Cincinnati to clinch the World Series.

9   The other school has a swimming pool with no team but we have a team and no pool.

10 If I told you we won the city title would you believe it?

Obey the signals / **COMMAS: YES OR NO?**

Substitute a *comma* in place of the blank space wherever required.

1   Last year I saw a man enter a cage full of lions __?__ and the only thing he carried was a whip.

2   Here come the winners: Jay __?__ Paul __?__ and Gilbert.

3   Do you prefer cake __?__ candy __?__ or fruit for dessert?

4   The P.T.A. elected a new president —?— vice-president —?— secretary —?— and treasurer for the coming year.

5   He tried hard —?— but he failed again.

6   Sometimes I wonder what it's like —?— at the bottom of the ocean.

7   Louis went to see the Knicks play at Madison Square Garden —?— New York City.

8   The freeways make traffic flow in Los Angeles —?— California.

9   I like your straight pitches —?— but I'm afraid of those curve balls.

10 Plants have strange names: clematis —?— calceolaria —?— cineraria —?— etc.

In This Lesson We Learned

- *Commas* are used to separate words in a series;
- after a long introductory clause;
- before *and/or/but* in a compound sentence;
- between numbers and names of places;
- in opening and closing a letter.

PUNCTUATION MARKS: USING THE SEMICOLON

When should you use the SEMICOLON?

RULES

⚠ **To separate two main clauses that could really be divided into two sentences.**

> The players looked weary and unhappy; they had just lost their first game of the season.

> *or:* The players looked weary and unhappy. They had just lost their first game of the season.

⚠ **To separate two parts of a sentence which already have used commas; thus, the semicolon shows the difference in parts.**

> The red-faced, angry referee scolded the noisy captain, the injured player, and the interfering coach; but the crowd in the grandstands loved every minute of it, cheering and shouting.

195

Stop and go / **COMMA AND SEMICOLON—I**

Re-write these sentences, putting semicolons and commas wherever required below.

1 Two men stood in the boxing ring one was the champion and the other was his opponent.

2 The crew stood ready to take off in their jet plane the pilot would not leave until the security officers checked all passengers.

3 Bakers make doughnuts crullers and bagels customers like these when fresh crisp and tasty.

4 You should always count your change sometimes storekeepers may make a mistake.

5 The parents were ready eager and impatient to get started on the trip the children gabbed giggled and delayed things.

Some sentences below require commas, some semicolons, and some both commas and semicolons. Rewrite and insert these punctuation marks wherever necessary.

1 Beauty shops for women do things to improve the looks of their hair skin and nails these are not so important as personality.

2 Geography books show pictures of mountains rivers and oceans these are the natural ways of dividing the land.

3 A jeweler displays rings watches and charms for sale and he will repair clocks bracelets and earrings for customers.

4 Play ball to the best of your ability win or lose be a sport.

5 When you go to a party go with someone you know that way you won't feel lonesome and strange.

6 She tried eating only proteins like meat fish and eggs for two weeks and she lost about twenty pounds.

7 The trouble with this kind of diet is that you must drink eight glasses of water a day that puts a strain on your kidneys.

8   One wise doctor said that the best way to lose weight is to stick a piece of tape across your mouth by this he meant no food no fat.

9   He was really teasing the patient you know that all you need to do is cut down on portions and do some walking.

10 Teen-agers who eat lettuce celery and other vegetables and have plenty of milk grow healthy look at their teeth eyes and complexion.

In This Lesson We Learned

The **semicolon** separates two main clauses. The semicolon separates two parts of a sentence already set off with commas.

REVIEW TESTS
IN PUNCTUATION

PUNCTUATION MARKS
ARE
STOPPING POINTS

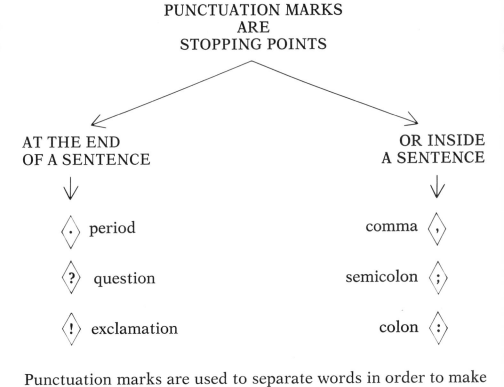

AT THE END
OF A SENTENCE

⟨.⟩ period

⟨?⟩ question

⟨!⟩ exclamation

OR INSIDE
A SENTENCE

comma ⟨,⟩

semicolon ⟨;⟩

colon ⟨:⟩

Punctuation marks are used to separate words in order to make
the meaning clear to the reader.

Punctuate this sketch of Andy Wims. Re-write the sentences.

ANDY WIMS

It's hard to pin a label on a guy like Andy Wims His official title at General Motors is Research Chemist Andy's a young scientist who's just designed a new device that will use lasers (pronounced "LAY'ZERS") and computers to improve ways of production He is studying a better method of painting for two reasons to reduce waste and to cut pollution by spraying

Andy's also a professional drummer not just the razzle-dazzle kind who plays the bongoes but a talented musician He can lay down the rock-rhythm needed to keep an orchestra together or he can carry along a small jazz group to entertain a college crowd

Is Andy Wims a chemist who plays drums or a drummer who plays with chemistry Both and more He's an interesting person doing good things on the job and he's a "pro" enjoying music in his spare time

---

TEST II

Punctuate each of these groups of words to make good sense. Re-write the sentences.

1 A hunter in darkest Africa had a frightening experience one day

2 He lost his guide wandered into the jungle and was surrounded by hostile natives

3 Suddenly he remembered a trick he had seen in an old silent movie

4 He reached in his pocket for his cigarette lighter pulled it out flicked it once and a big flame popped up

5 When you fly to Ireland your plane lands in Shannon

6 Which kind of story do you prefer mystery adventure or love

7 Come to my house tonight we will play chess after supper

8 There are styles for everyone tall short fat and thin

9 How many times must I tell you to stop bothering her

10 Hail hail the gang's all here

TEST III

Write the correct punctuation marks for the following sentences. Some are questions; others are answers. Re-write the sentences.

1 I would like a preparation of phenylisothiocyanate

2 Do you mean mustard oil

3 Yes I just can never think of that name

4 Do you know a good definition for alimony

5 Surely it is the high cost of leaving

6 Is that supposed to be a joke

7   It's not exactly a bit of chuckle-bait

8   But can you do any better

9   I'll say so any time

10   That stale joke was born a hundred years ago

Note: There are **3** ways of setting off an expression.
   A   **Quotation marks**   ⟶   "mustard oil"
   B   **Underlining**   ⟶   mustard oil
   C   **Italics**   ⟶   *mustard oil*

CAPITALIZATION

Capital letters stand out. They draw attention. They look more important. Your eye picks them out on a printed page. Your brain tells you that they are used for special persons, places, and things. They are not only a way of pointing out, but also a way of labeling things that are somehow special. You have already noticed capital letters in your own name, in books, in store windows, in newspapers, on street signs, and in many other places. To help you review, study the following rules as a guide for your own writing.

Capitalization Rules

(1) Names

PEOPLE —Governor Smith, Reverend Brown,
       Miss Quinn

PLACES —Maine, East River, Harlem, San Juan, Boston

THINGS—the Queen Elizabeth, the Statue of Liberty,
       Aquarius

(2) Famous Things

EVENTS —World's Fair, Civil War, the Gold Rush

BUILDINGS—Tower of London, World Trade Center, Empire
       State Building

SOCIETIES —Rotary Club, Democratic Party, Republican
       Party, the Red Cross

Dates

DAYS OF THE WEEK —Monday, Tuesday, Wednesday, Thursday, Friday, etc.

MONTHS —January, February, March, April, etc.

HOLIDAYS —New Year's Day, Easter, Labor Day, Thanksgiving

4 **Publications**

BOOKS —David Copperfield, Treasure Island, The Heart Is a Lonely Hunter

NEWSPAPERS—New York Times, Manchester Guardian, Chicago Tribune

MAGAZINES —Time, Newsweek, Mademoiselle, Sports Illustrated

5 **First Word**

SENTENCE —A boy put his finger in a hole to save the dike.

LINE OF POETRY —For thy sweet love rememb'red such wealth brings That then I scorn to change my state with kings.

QUOTATION—Franklin said, "A penny saved is a penny earned."

CAPITALIZATION EXERCISES

A Capitalize the words that need to be emphasized according to the five rules given previously. Re-write the sentences.

1 have you read "a history of the english speaking people" by winston churchill?

2 boys enjoy "life on the mississippi" by mark twain.

3 we always celebrate thanksgiving on the last thursday in november.

4 the members of the rotary club donated an ambulance to richmond hospital.

5   if you like fashions for girls, look at "seventeen" or "made-moiselle."

6   the bible says, "blessed are the peacemakers for they shall see god."

7   in europe we visited london, paris, rome, madrid, and other cities.

8   we saw the olympic stadium in tokyo, japan, last year.

9   the empire state building is not so tall as the world trade center.

10   the indians named the delaware river, but they have long ago vanished.

B   Answer these questions, using *capitals* wherever needed.

1   Which day follows Saturday?

2   What is the rock at the southern tip of Spain?

3   Which continent is called "down under" the equator?

4   Can you name the discoverer of the West Indies?

5   Do you know who invented the electric light bulb?

6   Who makes the laws for the United States?

7   Which city is the capital of England?

8   "Old Faithful" is a natural geyser in which park out West?

9   Name the showplace for tourists and children in Florida?

10   Where do all the nations meet to discuss world problems?

C Give an example of each of these requiring *capital* letters.

1 Your local newspaper?

2 The largest department store in your town?

3 The name and position of the number one citizen of your town?

4 A historical showplace you have visited?

5 Your favorite TV program?

6 The brand of coffee or tea your family uses?

7 The title of a book you read recently?

8 The name of the college you would some day like to attend?

9 Your favorite baseball team?

10 Your favorite football team?

In This Lesson We Learned

Capitals are used to show the reader which persons, places, and things have special rank or importance.

In the days of beautiful handwriting before the invention of the printing press, the monks in the monasteries used to pay devoted attention to capital letters by decorating them with artistic designs in gold and color.

SPELLING

A—B—C=ALWAYS BE CAREFUL!

There are over half a million words in the English language. You don't have to know them all. Just make sure you can spell the words *you use!* Follow these suggestions and keep track of the right spelling of any words that you have missed. Start a section in your English notebook with the heading My Own Spelling List *or* Words I Must Know.

HOW TO LEARN TO SPELL IN 5 EASY STEPS

The best way is "see and say." And then
if you do it right, you can "spell and write."

SEE THE WORD.	**Look carefully!** pickle (ends *le*) but nickel (ends *el*)
SAY THE WORD.	**Watch out for silent letters!** soften (silent *t*) and plumber (silent *b*)
SPELL THE WORD.	**Whisper it softly!** f-o-r-e-i-g-n-e-r (meaning "a stranger")
WRITE THE WORD.	**Take it easy!** quarter (25¢) (notice *r* before *t*)
CHECK THE WORD.	**Compare with the dictionary.** truly (there is no *e*)

WHICH WORDS MUST YOU KNOW?

Experience has shown that there are about 100 basic words used in everyday friendly letters and business writing. Do you know how to spell these words 100% perfectly? Follow the five easy steps or else have a class "buddy" try them with you. Study the ones you miss. Re-test yourself. Do it again until you have mastered the list. You can—if you really try!

100 Basic Words

ache	done	making	they
again	don't	many	though
always	early	meant	through
among	easy	minute	tired
answer	enough	much	tonight
any	every	none	too
been	February	often	trouble
beginning	forty	once	truly
believe	friend	piece	Tuesday
blue	grammar	raise	two
break	guess	read	used
built	half	ready	very
business	having	said	wear
busy	hear	says	Wednesday
buy	heard	seems	week
can't	here	separate	where
choose	hoarse	shoes	whether
color	hour	since	which
coming	instead	some	whole
cough	just	straight	women
could	knew	sugar	won't
country	know	sure	would
dear	laid	tear	write
doctor	loose	their	writing
doesn't	lose	there	wrote

SEE THE WORD / CHECK / WRITE / SPELL

Take your time when spelling / **SPELLING QUIZ**

Write these words correctly to fit the meaning.

1 Name of the month following January? F__?__ Y

2 Name of the day following Tuesday? W __?__ Y

3 The study of the rules of language? G __?__ R

4 One's trade or occupation? B __?__ S

5 To put apart, or divide? S __?__ E

6 To be without something and not know where it is? L __?__ E

7 Starting, or taking the first step? B __?__ G

8 In the middle of things, or surrounded by? A __?__ G

9 Moving toward; arriving; approaching? C __?__ G

10 Without a bend; direct; not crooked or curved? S __?__ T

Now check your spelling with the previous word list.

See the word in your mind before spelling it / **PUZZLES**

Can you figure these out?

1 Do these words need the letter *e* or no letter in the space?

make	mak — ing	raise	rais — ing
choose	choos — ing	skate	skat — ing
have	hav — ing	rinse	rins — ing
lose	los — ing	squeeze	squeez — ing
write	writ — ing	slide	slid — ing

M A K E + I N G

= M A K   I N G

2 Do you put *ei* or *ie* in the blanks to complete these words?

bel — — ve   rec — — ve

fr — — nd   n — — ghbor

p — — ce   w — — gh

3 Where do you put the apostrophe in these words?

cannot	=	cant
do not	=	dont
will not	=	wont
could not	=	couldnt
does not	=	doesnt
did not	=	didnt

REMEMBER
NOT = N'T

4 Spell the words that sound like the samples given below.

SOUND		WORD	MEANING
off	=	c — — — —	(wheeze)
cuff	=	en — — — —	(sufficient)
oh	=	th — — — —	(even if)
blue	=	thr — — — —	(all the way)
how	=	b — — — —	(branch)

5 Write the double letters to fit the number of spaces below.

to select   =   to ch — — se

not tied   =   l — — se

appears	=	s——ms
seven days	=	one w——k
to happen	=	to o——ur
a mistake	=	an e——or

Only 100% counts here / **SPELLING DICTATION TEST**

The following is to be read by the teacher or a pupil to the class. The selection contains words from the list of 100 Basic Words.

One Tuesday in the beginning of February, a tired country doctor who was about forty wrote to his dear friend. He said that, though he knew the women were very busy, he believed they would know that it would not be too much trouble for them to come early Wednesday to the house he had built when he received his first raise.

It's true there was some business he had meant to finish for many weeks. He was sure that he would be ready to answer truly, with no mistakes in grammar, every easy question they laid before him, within an hour of their coming.

Having done this, he just put on the blue slippers that he always used to wear so he won't become hoarse and went straight to the closet where he separated half the loose sugar. He was careful, too, not to let anything tear or slip through his fingers and break into pieces. I guess he doesn't want to buy any again.

I hear that, since the women were having a merry time here making colors, when they heard what the doctor wanted they stopped for a whole minute. They were led to write that they had read his note and had hoped he would lose his cough and ache tonight.

In This Lesson We Learned

Spelling the 100 basic words depends on *careful* steps:

SEE, SAY, SPELL, WRITE, CHECK.

Always Be Careful! (*A—B—C.*)

SPELLING RULES

The best rule for spelling is, *"When in doubt, leave it out—or look it up!"*

There are a few rules that may help you. The only trouble is the fact that some words are called "exceptions" because they don't follow the rules. The only sure way of checking any word is to look it up in a dictionary.

RULE I

Drop the final *e* when adding *able*.

    desire + able = desirable
    move   + able = movable
    value   + able = valuable
    use   + able = usable

Exceptions:

Keep the final *e* when adding *able*, if the word ends in *ce* or *ge*.

    notice + able = noticeable
    service + able = serviceable
    change + able = changeable
    dredge + able = dredgeable

RULE II

Drop the final *e* when adding *ing*.

    take   + ing = taking
    freeze + ing = freezing
    dine   + ing = dining
    give   + ing = giving

No exceptions!

Rules help you spell / **USING RULES I AND II**

Spell the words below, adding *able* or *ing*. Do you drop the final *e* or keep it? Study Rule I and Rule II to be sure!

1	blame	+	able	*11*	come	+	ing
2	receive	+	able	*12*	write	+	ing
3	love	+	able	*13*	make	+	ing
4	advise	+	able	*14*	pierce	+	ing
5	debate	+	able	*15*	save	+	ing
6	peace	+	able	*16*	fence	+	ing
7	trace	+	able	*17*	bake	+	ing
8	manage	+	able	*18*	ride	+	ing
9	arrange	+	able	*19*	mine	+	ing
10	exchange	+	able	*20*	pave	+	ing

RULE III

Double the final letter of *short words* (*one* syllable) having at the end a single consonant, preceded by a single vowel. You double the last letter before adding *ing* or *ed*.

SHORT WORD	ING ADDED	ED ADDED
stop	stopping	stopped
rip	ripping	ripped
tan	tanning	tanned
strum	strumming	strummed
bat	batting	batted
drop	dropping	dropped
slap	slapping	slapped
rub	rubbing	rubbed
fan	fanning	fanned
slip	slipping	slipped

Vowels are A, E, I, O, U.
Consonants are the remaining letters.

RULE IV

Double the final letter of *long words* **(** *two* **or more syllables) having at the end a single consonant, preceded by a single vowel, and accent (or stress) on the ending. Double before** *ing* **or** *ed.*

LONG WORD	ING ADDED	ED ADDED
prefer	preferring	preferred
occur	occurring	occurred
patrol	patrolling	patrolled
transfer	transferring	transferred
submit	submitting	submitted
regret	regretting	regretted
permit	permitting	permitted
admit	admitting	admitted
equip	equipping	equipped
dispel	dispelling	dispelled

A rule a day keeps errors away! / **USING RULES III AND IV**

Spell out the word that fits the sentence.

1 Our teacher said, "No run—ing through the halls!"

2 We were permit—ed to go out during lunch time.

3 New cars come equip—ed with safety belts.

4 After a summer on the beach, she looked all tan—ed.

5 She lost her balance and slip—ed on the icy street.

6 He loved singing along while strum—ing his guitar.

7 They lost some time while transfer—ing the records.

214

Spelling rules fix your attention on certain regular changes made in words and also point out the troublesome exceptions.

8 Boys carrying palm branches were fan—ing the tribal chief.

9 During a slump, his bat—ing average went down.

10 I heard a sound of rip—ing as my coat caught on a nail.

11 We would have prefer—ed going to the early show.

12 She accused her neighbor's daughter of slap—ing her face.

13 You must pay a deposit when submit—ing your application.

14 To avoid any mistake, we stop—ed to ask for directions.

15 The bright warm sun quickly dispel—ed the morning fog.

16 Yesterday an accident occur—ed at the ramp to the bridge.

17 She really regret—ed all those unnecessary remarks.

18   The coach admit—ed him because he was trying so hard.

19   Forget—ing to turn her watch ahead one hour, Mary was late to class.

20   To stimulate circulation, use some rub—ing salve on the bruise.

In This Lesson We Learned

Spelling rules are helpful.

- **Drop** final *e* when adding *able* or *ing*.
- **Double** final letter before adding *ing* or *ed*.

Watch out for the exceptions or words that do not follow the rules. When in doubt, check with the dictionary.

HOW TO SPELL
WITH NO MISTAKES

Somewhere in your notebook keep a list of the words you find troublesome.

I saw a pupil in a science class correctly spell a difficult word (*metamorphosis* = "change of form of an animal"), yet he blundered on an easy word (*label* = "sign"). Why? Probably, long words force you to pay attention to all the letters; short words you just guess. **You need care in seeing, saying, and writing.** You can avoid common errors by really trying for 100% correctness. Here are some helpful suggestions.

1   Watch what happens when you add something at the *beginning* of these words. This is called a ***prefix.***

PREFIX		WORD		
un	+	necessary	=	unnecessary
ir	+	responsible	=	irresponsible
pre	+	exist	=	preexist
mis	+	spelling	=	misspelling
dis	+	satisfied	=	dissatisfied
re	+	elect	=	reelect
im	+	moral	=	immoral

2 Notice the double letters when you add something at the *end* of these words. This is called a *suffix*.

WORD		SUFFIX		
usual	+	ly	=	usually
natural	+	ly	=	naturally
accidental	+	ly	=	accidentally
incidental	+	ly	=	incidentally
mean	+	ness	=	meanness
keen	+	ness	=	keenness

3 Observe the *silent* letters which must be written, though not spoken.

wrestling has a silent *w* and *t*
plumbing has a silent *b*
meant has a silent *a*
soften has a silent *t*
knock has a silent *k* and *c*

These should be seen, not heard.

4 Beware of words that sound alike. These are called **homonyms**.

blue (color)
blew (sounded)

horse (animal)
hoarse (muffled)

peace (quiet)
piece (chunk)

"He spends his school days in a daze."

wait (stay)
weight (heaviness)

seen (observed)
scene (location)

too (very)
to (in the direction of)

5 Learn the various *sounds* that some letters have when spoken.

c	has the sound of s	in poli*c*e
c	has the sound of sh	in pre*c*ious
c	has the sound of k	in *c*andy
qu	has the sound of kw	in *qu*estion
s	has the sound of z	in becau*s*e
ti	has the sound of sh	in na*ti*on
x	has the sound of z	in *x*ylophone
x	has the sound of gz	in e*x*amination

218

6 Don't add *extra* sounds and extra letters to words.

RIGHT   WRONG

umbrella   *not* umbErella
athlete   *not* athAlete
idea   *not* ideaR
mischievous   *not* mischEVIous
perspiration   *not* pREspiration
chimney   *not* chimIney

SPELLING EXERCISES

A Add the *prefixes* and spell the words correctly.

un + noticed =

dis + appear =

Don't drop or add any letters.

pre + cooked =

mis + step =

ir + resistible =

re + enforce =

im + mortal =

B Add the *suffixes* and spell the words correctly.

final + ly =

actual + ly =

Watch the double letters.

real + ly =

open + ness =

good + ness =

hope + less =

C   Write the *silent* letters which we spell but do not say.

safety = s-a-f-e-t-y

weight = w-e-i-g-h-t

coarse = c-o-a-r-s-e

bottle = b-o-t-t-l-e

giggle = g-i-g-g-l-e

listen = l-i-s-t-e-n

D   Write the *extra* letters which do not belong in these words. Spell each word correctly.

One too many!

allready	equiptment
hungary	chiminey
bannana	athalete
worser	umberella
disasterous	truely

E   Spell the correct word that sounds like the one given in italics in these expressions. Be sure it fits the meaning.

1   All the policemen, dressed in *blew*, paraded.

2   Please let me have a *peace* of bread.

3   You should have *scene* the field after the game.

4   She says she is watching her *wait*.

5   Can you pick the best *hoarse* in the next race?

F   Write these sentences, correctly spelling each word as dictated by your teacher or classmate.

1   Your good name is your most *precious* thing.

2   Some razor blades have an extra *keenness*.

3   Can you play the *xylophone* or the harmonica?

4   If you want to go to the beach you must be good, or it's out of the *question*.

5   If you feel *too* tired, you better take a rest now.

In This Lesson We Learned

To spell with no mistakes, you must be careful of such things as the prefix, suffix, silent letters, and "sound alikes." Check with the dictionary!

When in doubt about the spelling of a word, look it up in the dictionary.

REVIEW TESTS IN SPELLING

TEST I

Write the complete word.

1 Twenty-five cents is a QUA ―?― ER of a dollar.

2 Strangers in a country are called FOR ―?― GNERS.

3 A business letter closes with "Yours TR ―?― LY."

4 The middle of the week is W ―?― ESDAY.

5 The second month of the year is FEB ―?― ARY.

6 A friend tried to SEP ―?― RATE the angry boys.

7 If you trust someone, you BEL ―?― VE him.

8 Can you walk a STR ―?― T line?

9 During the springtime we have rainy W ―?― THER.

10 Sometimes it really DO ―?― N'T make any difference.

TEST II

Some words drop the final *e*; some keep the final *e*. Write these words correctly.

1	squeeze	+	ing	=	6	notice	+	able	=
2	choose	+	ing	=	7	come	+	ing	=
3	love	+	able	=	8	bake	+	ing	=
4	force	+	ible	=	9	move	+	able	=
5	peace	+	able	=	10	use	+	able	=

TEST III

Some words *double* the final letter before adding a suffix. Write the correct spelling for the following words according to the sample below.

	WORD	WORD + ING	WORD + ED
1	stop	stopping	stopped
2	slip		
3	drop		
4	rub		
5	part		
6	invent		
7	admit		
8	prefer		
9	occur		
10	beg		

TEST IV

When adding a *prefix* (at the beginning) or a *suffix* (at the end), be very careful of the spelling of the new word. Complete the following.

1	dis + appoint =	
2	un + natural =	
3	re + print =	
4	mis + match =	
5	pre + judge =	
6	sub + way =	
7	in + accurate =	
8	im + possible =	
9	bi + weekly =	
10	non + sense =	

11	usual + ly =	
12	keen + ness =	
13	act + or =	
14	equal + ly =	
15	sudden + ness =	
16	debt + or =	
17	employ + ee =	
18	critic + ize =	
19	question + aire =	
20	science + ist =	

If you master some of the word-elements that occur frequently in English words (prefixes and suffixes), you will soon find the key that unlocks the meaning of thousands of words.

TEST V

Either the instructor or a class "buddy" may dictate this test. The sentence makes clear the use of the word.

1	**suggest**	Will you *suggest* a workable plan?
2	**meant**	The man *meant* well.
3	**folks**	He will visit his old *folks*.
4	**absence**	Her *absence* was caused by illness.
5	**ought**	You *ought* to have known better.
6	**recent**	The river rose during the *recent* storm.
7	**national**	Wilbur won the *national* spelling bee.
8	**decide**	The judge will *decide* the case.
9	**receive**	It is better to give than to *receive*.
10	**occupy**	They will soon *occupy* their new house.
11	**colonies**	The *colonies* fought for freedom.
12	**proceed**	Mary will *proceed* according to instructions.
13	**athletic**	To be *athletic* is a sign of good health.
14	**sincerely**	He spoke to the crowd quite *sincerely*.
15	**practical**	The carpenter drew a *practical* sketch.
16	**majority**	A *majority* vote is needed to win the election.
17	**beginning**	In the *beginning*, there was nothing.
18	**expense**	The bridge was built at great *expense*.
19	**relief**	The medicine gave her some *relief* from pain.
20	**cordially**	You are *cordially* invited to come to our party.
21	**February**	The shortest month of the year is *February*.
22	**character**	You judge a man's *character* by his deeds.
23	**business**	Please, mind your own *business*.
24	**accept**	We *accept* your invitation with pleasure.
25	**various**	The city may be reached by *various* highways.
26	**accident**	The car was damaged in an *accident*.

27	volume	Please turn down the *volume* on the T.V.
28	guess	Can you *guess* how much that boy weighs?
29	argument	Please stop this useless *argument*.
30	invitation	Why don't you reply to the *invitation*?
31	minute	Will you wait just one more *minute*?
32	whose	*Whose* shoes are you wearing now?
33	really	I don't believe they are *really* yours.
34	earliest	The janitor always comes in *earliest*.
35	probably	It will *probably* rain tomorrow.
36	foreign	My son collects *foreign* coins as a hobby.
37	scene	A street *scene* in Naples is very colorful.
38	develop	Take pictures when traveling, but *develop* them here.
39	finally	That's how we *finally* got our snapshots.
40	whether	I wonder *whether* the sun is shining in Vermont.
41	citizen	A person born here is an American *citizen*.
42	divide	The Mississippi River can almost *divide* the country.
43	discussion	A good *discussion* requires the give and take of ideas.
44	principal	The teachers gave the retiring *principal* a gold watch.
45	height	An elevator rises to the *height* of the building.
46	secretary	My *secretary* is the best in the whole system.
47	association	You must pay dues when you join the *association*.
48	session	At each *session* of Congress, a prayer is said.
49	reference	A good letter of *reference* helps get a job.
50	appreciate	I *appreciate* all the kind things you do for me.

WORD-GAMES

Have you ever played *Scrabble? Keyword?* Good fun.

Try this word-game offering you three kinds of pieces:

    the *beginning* of a word   (called the ***prefix***)
    the *middle* of a word   (called the ***stem***)
    the *ending* of a word   (called the ***suffix***)

All you need to do is put together those pieces that make a word and then check with your dictionary. For example:

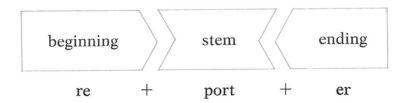

      re   +   port   +   er

These three pieces put together = **reporter.** The dictionary tells you the meaning of *reporter:* "one who gathers news for a newspaper."

    Can you put the pieces together? In the exercises that follow there are some useful prefixes, stems, and suffixes to form words.

227

WORD-GAMES BUILD VOCABULARY

A   Write the complete word and its meaning.

re	+	use	=
re	+	sale	=
re	+	view	=
re	+	call	=
re	+	fuel	=

un	+	natural	=
un	+	clear	=
un	+	touched	=
un	+	known	=
un	+	heard	=

dis	+	agree	=
dis	+	appoint	=
dis	+	cover	=
dis	+	loyal	=
dis	+	prove	=

| hope | + | ful | = |
| peace | + | ful | = |

care + ful =

doubt + ful =

grate + ful =

*Drop the silent _e_ before adding _able_ in the starred words.

*move + able =

honor + able =

*live + able =

eat + able =

drink + able =

*re + move + able =

un + grate + ful =

dis + honor + able =

*re + use + able =

dis + grace + ful =

B Write the complete word and its meaning.

in + active =

in + direct =

in + complete =

in + sufficient =

in + effective =

229

bi	+	cycle	=
bi	+	weekly	=
bi	+	monthly	=
bi	+	lingual	=
bi	+	partisan	=

trans	+	plant	=
trans	+	form	=
trans	+	late	=
trans	+	fusion	=
trans	+	Atlantic	=

pre	+	fab	=
pre	+	cooked	=
pre	+	stamped	=
pre	+	finished	=
pre	+	school	=

non	+	sense	=
non	+	smoker	=
non	+	voting	=
non	+	working	=
non	+	appearance	=

Can you label the parts of the alligator prefix, stem and suffix ?

C Write the meaning of the word elements below. For example: *anti* means "against" as in the word "antiwar."

re   means __?__ as in renew

un   means __?__ as in unimportant

dis   means __?__ as in dissatisfied

ful   means __?__ as in dutiful

able   means __?__ as in recognizable

in   means __?__ as in infamous

bi   means __?__ as in binoculars

trans   means __?__ as in transocean

pre   means __?__ as in pretested

non   means __?__ as in nonresident

FOR EXTRA CREDIT

Using the 10 word elements given in Part C, prepare a list of 10 other words not already used in this lesson. Give their meaning.

Bring **SCRABBLE** or **KEYWORD** to class for a contest in words!

In This Lesson We Learned

Word-games help build vocabulary. Words may be put together by using *prefixes,* *stems,* and *suffixes.* These are very useful in figuring out the meaning of words.

SYNONYMS

When you make a mistake, what kind of error would you call it?

A blunder / a boner / a blooper / a fumble / a slip / or whatever?

It depends on how serious or how foolish your mistake, and your choice of word shows how strongly you feel about it.

Synonyms are words having the same meaning. That is, they carry the same general idea, but say it just a bit differently to show there is some variation.

Do you know any synonyms for *hat?* As you know, the dictionary says: "a hat is a shaped covering for the head, usually with a crown and a brim, worn outdoors." Here are a few, just to show you that, although they all cover the head, they each have a difference. Notice the shape, the material, the style, etc.

cap	for baseball player out in the field, not at bat
cowl	for football player while sitting on bench
hood	for young lady wearing a cape with hood attached
helmet	for soldier, fireman, motorcyclist; hard metal cover
beret	for artist or traveler abroad; soft cloth, no brim
derby	for sport or dandy; stiff black felt in shape of bowl
fedora	for gentleman; soft felt hat with curled brim
shako	for member of a marching band; plumes on top
ski mask	for ski enthusiast to protect head and face in cold
mortarboard	for graduate, wearing gown at ceremony

Can you think of other hats? Daniel Boone wore a *coonskin cap;* a cardinal of the Church wears a red *biretta;* a rabbi wears a *yomulka* or black skullcap; a naughty boy wears a *dunce cap!*

233

Hit the mark / **SYNONYMS: WORDS HAVING THE SAME MEANING**

Select the correct *synonym* for the italicized word in each case.

1 Because of the high heels, she walked a bit *awkwardly*.
(noisily, riskily, stiffly, softly)

2 The busy traffic made that corner crossing *perilous*.
(safe, dangerous, dizzying, slow-moving)

3 After the *abundant* harvest, apples became much cheaper.
(skimpy, autumn, rainy, plentiful)

4 Try not to *provoke* the animals by poking them.
(touch, excite, feed, tickle)

5 If you *deviate* from these directions, you may get lost.
(turn, follow, destroy, forget)

6 The jeweler set the hands of the watch at the *precise* time.
(exact, wrong, approximate, nearest)

7 The FBI agent received praise for his *exploit*.
(discovery, arrest, suspicion, brave deed)

8 When you are young, you take more *risks* without worrying.
(chances, losses, gains, setbacks)

9 The bank teller spotted the *counterfeit* twenty dollar bill.
(genuine, antique, sham, worn-out)

10 On the telephone, she spoke *vivaciously* to her girlfriend.
(sadly, animatedly, sluggishly, angrily)

FOR EXTRA CREDIT

In brief descriptions, tell the differences in these kinds of footgear.

slippers	clogs	sneakers	boots
sandals	pumps	mules	rubbers
oxfords	wedgies	saddles	galoshes

Use a variety of synonyms to make your writing more vivid and colorful.

LIST OF USEFUL SYNONYMS

Learn to use these correctly. Look in the dictionary for the meaning!

NOUNS AND VERBS

1	*game*	→	contest	pastime	sport
2	*fight*	→	struggle	scuffle	tussle
3	*leave*	→	depart	retreat	retire
4	*ask*	→	request	demand	beg
5	*refuse*	→	reject	spurn	decline
6	*help*	→	aid	assist	support
7	*rush*	→	hurry	dash	speed
8	*scream*	→	shriek	screech	cry out
9	*laugh*	→	chuckle	giggle	smile
10	*unite*	→	join	combine	merge

ADJECTIVES AND ADVERBS

11	*happy*	→	cheerful	glad	joyous
12	*tired*	→	weary	exhausted	run-down
13	*eager*	→	keen	fervent	ardent
14	*stingy*	→	scanty	skimpy	miserly
15	*brave*	→	bold	fearless	confident
16	*roughly*	→	ruggedly	crudely	harshly
17	*kindly*	→	gently	mildly	cordially
18	*terribly*	→	frightfully	dreadfully	awfully
19	*suddenly*	→	quickly	abruptly	unexpectedly
20	*quietly*	→	silently	peacefully	noiselessly

FOR EXTRA CREDIT

Go to the school library and borrow Webster's DICTIONARY OF SYNONYMS AND ANTONYMS. Find the explanation given for any 5 of the words listed above. Use your notebook.

Enrich your vocabulary / **USE SYNONYMS FOR VARIETY**

Write a *synonym* taken from the LIST OF USEFUL SYNO-NYMS that fits the meaning in each sentence below.

1   Every time she heard a joke, she would (LAUGH) as if she really enjoyed it.

2   The students collected signatures to (ASK) permission to have a picnic.

3   To develop physical fitness and learn how to get along with others, join a team and take part in (GAMES).

4   The makers of breakfast cereals appear to (UNITE) their efforts in setting prices for various foods.

5   Always let your parents know where you are going and let them know before you (LEAVE).

6   The shock value of a mystery story depends on how (SUDDENLY) the crime is committed.

7   The solution to the problem sometimes comes after two hundred pages when the reader grows (TIRED).

8   Young girls like boys who do not treat them poorly or (ROUGHLY).

9   The girls on the cheering squad were so (EAGER) that the fans in the stands applauded their antics.

10   The nurse handled the injured boy so (QUIETLY) that he soon stopped crying and watched her bandage his leg.

Score well / **MATCH THE SYNONYMS**

Choose the correct synonym or word having the same meaning as the word in bold type given at the beginning of each group. For example:

    regret   →   forget / remember / <u>feel sad</u>

1 **rigid**   →   cold / angry / stiff

2 **slumber**   →   mumble / sleep /tumble

3 **conquer**   →   lose / surrender / win

4 **disgrace**   →   mistake / anger / shame

5 **relief**   →   sigh / comfort / pain

6 **provoke**   →   stir up / bring back / set forth

7 **automatic**   →   quick / self-moving / fixed

8 **genuine**   →   valuable / antique / natural

9 **solemn**   →   heavy / serious / quiet

10 **sturdy**   →   short / weak / strong

FOR EXTRA CREDIT

Write original sentences using 10 synonyms found in the list above.

In This Lesson We Learned

Synonyms are words having almost the same meaning. Use them for interesting *variety* in speaking and writing.

ANTONYMS

We learn from our own experience that the world around us is full of opposites. That is why we have words in opposite pairs. For example, here are some everyday *antonyms*, or words that are *opposite* in meaning.

hot/cold	forget/remember
true/false	lose/find
strong/weak	repair/damage
old/young	agree/disagree
new/old	tense/relaxed

Warm up / **ANTONYMS—I**

Can you tell at a glance which of these sets of words are *opposite* in meaning? Write YES if opposite.

1 generous / stingy   4 allow / forbid

2 reward / punish   5 foulness / pollution

3 identify / know

You should have written YES for 3 of these 5 sets.

Aim; steady; fire! / **ANTONYMS—II**

Try this little quiz. Write the *opposites*. Get 5 out of 5.

The *opposite* of beautiful is   ugly / lovely / expensive

The *opposite* of obedient is   sly / unruly / dutiful

The *opposite* of brilliant is   bright / steady / dull

The *opposite* of faithful is   fickle / loyal / dependable

The *opposite* of profit is   gain / surplus / loss

Take your distance / **ANTONYMS—III**

When you use an antonym for a word, you have the opposite meaning. For example, you can turn the whole meaning of a sentence around by changing just one word.

SAMPLE: I'm *glad* you came.
   I'm *sorry* you came.

Write an *antonym* in place of the italicized word. Notice how the meaning changes!

1   In the last few minutes of play, we *won* the game.

2   Around midnight, the rain *stopped*.

3   She looked very *sad* when we first met her.

4   The fertilizer made the grass get *weaker*.

5   At the scheduled time, the plane *landed*.

6   Every month, he *withdrew* some money.

7   The painter said he wanted to use *separate* colors.

8 Just before supper, we felt *satisfied*.

9 Myles said, "I'd rather *run*."

10 With good friends, you can *remember* your troubles.

Hit the mark / **ANTONYMS—IV**

Using some of the *antonyms* listed below, write the ones that complete the meaning of the sentences.

handsome	/	ugly	unknown	/	famous
summer	/	winter	weak	/	powerful
quickly	/	slowly	warlike	/	peaceful
display	/	conceal	sunshine	/	rain
selfish	/	generous	sweet	/	sour
appear	/	vanish	work	/	play
genuine	/	false	question	/	answer
growing	/	shrinking	spend	/	save
borrow	/	return	honor	/	disgrace
cash	/	credit	build	/	destroy

SENTENCES

1 An __?__ person may some day become __?__ because of good

deeds.

2 Whenever you __?__ something from a friend, you should

__?__ it in the same condition.

3 The Delaware Indians were a __?__ tribe, not savage and wild

as the __?__ Iroquois tribe.

4 Do you remember the story of the __?__ duckling that grew

into a __?__ swan?

240

5   In the beginning, Scrooge was a __?__ character, but at the end of "A Christmas Carol" he became __?__.

6   Bank tellers who handle money must learn how to tell __?__ dollar bills from counterfeit or __?__ money.

7   When you are young, your bones are __?__; but in old age your bones start __?__.

8   Instead of paying __?__ for purchases, shoppers are using __?__ cards to avoid carrying money.

9   We build monuments to __?__ men like Lincoln and Washington, but nothing for traitors like Benedict Arnold who fell into __?__.

10 When you watch a magician do card tricks, you can easily see what he wants to __?__, but you can never figure out how he can __?__ a card.

Take another step forward / **ANTONYMS—V**

Complete the statement by writing the word that fits the meaning. Study the clues; use a dictionary to find the words you need.

1   In the darkness, familiar things look **s (5) e.**
    clues: unusual, different, not recognizable

2   Whether you are a beginner or a **v (5) n,** you must obey the rules.
    clues: an older and more experienced person

3 Business has its ups and downs, commonly called "booms" and **"b (3) s."**

    clues: slowdown periods or depressions

4 England expects every man to do his **d (2) y,** not whatever he feels like.

    clues: job or whatever he is supposed to do

5 Walking through the woods, you hear not sounds, but only **s (5) e.**

    clues: quiet, unmoving things

Now for the next round / **ANTONYMS—VI**

For each word in Column *A,* write the *letter* of its antonym (opposite) in Column *B.*

COLUMN A		COLUMN B	
1	busy	*a*	joy
2	sadness	*b*	lazy
3	success	*c*	unprepared
4	guilty	*d*	ignorance
5	knowledge	*e*	defeat
6	tidy	*f*	rude
7	question	*g*	innocent
8	ready	*h*	answer
9	courteous	*i*	dear
10	cheap	*j*	unclean

Write the word that is *opposite* in meaning to the first word in each line below.

1 **rough** → gentle / harsh / tough

2 **tactful** → polite / rude / friendly

3 **attentive** → interested / alert / disregarding

4 **private** → personal / selfish / public

5 **distinct** → fuzzy / clear / sharp

6 **loud** → noisy / soft / annoying

7 **healthy** → sickly / well / vigorous

8 **bold** → shy / brave / dashing

9 **calm** → neat / nervous / cool

10 **recent** → new / cheap / old

In This Lesson We Learned

Antonyms are words opposite in meaning. Examples: rich, poor / dead, alive / good, bad / fancy, plain.

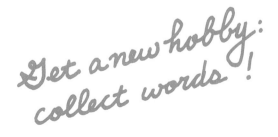
Get a new hobby: collect words!

NAME-WORDS FROM PEOPLE/ PLACES/ THINGS

Be a word-detective! Track down the origins of English words. You will find that they come from various sources. Some words come from names of people; some from places; others from things. They are all an interesting record of how a living language grows. Here are a few samples to show you where we have made up or borrowed words in order to give a name to something.

I. Words From Names of People

Find the meanings in the dictionary.

	WORD	NAME OF PERSON	NATIONALITY
1	pasteurize	Louis Pasteur	French
2	volt	Alessandro Volta	Italian
3	watt	James Watt	British
4	boycott	Captain Boycott	Irish
5	dahlia	Adolph Dahl	Swedish
6	guillotine	Dr. Guillotin	French
7	bowie knife	James Bowie	American
8	nicotine	Jean Nicot	French
9	pap test	Dr. George Papanicolaou	Greek
10	salk vaccine	Dr. Jonas Salk	American

The lives of great men are worthy of study.

Write the *number* of the name–word in the previous list that matches the correct definition below.

a. tobacco juice poison

b. device for beheading

c. flower

d. germ-killing process

e. test for cancer

f. electrical power delivered

g. preventive against "polio"

h. weapon for hand fighting

i. refusal to buy goods

j. electricity used by bulb, etc.

MORE WORDS FROM PEOPLE'S NAMES

You will find a bit of history associated with some words from people's names. Somebody discovered a new process, and his name became the word for the process.

mesmerize from Dr. Mesmer, a German doctor, who used to hypnotize his patients; therefore, mesmerize means *hypnotize.*

macadam from McAdam, a Scottish inventor, who first used broken stone to make a road; therefore, macadam means a road or pavement made of *layers of broken stone.*

245

lynch	from Captain Lynch of Virginia, who was the author of a law regarding punishment by death for an offense without a trial; therefore, lynch means *death by hanging* by private persons without authority.
fox trot	from a dance instructor named Fox; it is a *social dance* for couples, using short quick steps in various combinations.
dunce	from Duns Scotus, a scholar, who was called dull-witted and stupid by his enemies; a dunce is a *numbskull*.
sandwich	from the Earl of Sandwich. He was too busy to sit down at a table and eat, so he asked for two slices of bread with some meat. A sandwich is *two slices of bread with any meat, cheese, fish, etc.* A "hero" is a loaf sandwich loaded with veal, peppers, etc.
Listerine	from Dr. Lister, a British surgeon, who was the first to use antiseptics during operations. Listerine is an *antiseptic* used for wounds, mouth wash, etc., to kill germs.
platonic	from Plato, a Greek philosopher and thinker who said true love is ideal; platonic means *ideal*.
sideburns	from General Burnside who had side whiskers and mustache, but shaved his chin. Sideburns means *side whiskers*.
vandyke	from Vandyke, a Flemish painter, who had a pointed beard at the chin. A vandyke means a *short pointed beard*.

What's the story? / **NAME-WORDS WITH A BIT OF HISTORY**

Write the word that correctly completes each of these sentences. Use the name–words given above.

1 The highway department decided to put black top over the

__?__ on the streets of our town.

2 At the annual picnic, we gave soda and a —?— to anyone who asked for them.

3 Some teenagers who sport long hair have even tried to grow —?— in the style of the Civil War general.

4 Whenever you have small cuts or abrasions, you better use an antiseptic solution, such as —?—.

5 If you try to read from notes instead of speaking to the class, you gradually become —?— by your notes.

II. Words From Names of Places

Check the meanings in the dictionary:

	WORD	PLACE
1	coffee	Caffa (Turkey)
2	tangerine	Tangiers (Africa)
3	hollyhock	Holy Land (Palestine)
4	calico	Calicut (India)
5	frankfurter	Frankfurt (Germany)
6	port (wine)	Oporto (Portugal)
7	champagne	Campagne (France)
8	milliner	Milan (Italy)
9	tariff	Tarifa (Spain)
10	copper	Cyprus (Mediterranean island)

Where and why? / **WORDS THAT COME FROM PLACES**

Match the above place-words with the right meanings below.

a. "hot dog"

b. sweet wine (red)

c. flower

d. orange (small mandarin)

e. metal

f. bubbly wine (white)

g. dress material (printed)

h. roasted bean juice

i. hat designer

j. tax or charge

III. Words From Trade-Names of Things

When new things are put on the market, they carry a brand name. After some years go by, the trade name drops into such common use that the thing is called by the original word, except that we spell it with a small letter. Here are a few examples for you to sudy.

1	**aspirin**	— headache and pain reliever tablets
2	**kleenex**	— clothlike tissue used as handkerchief
3	**kodak**	— small portable camera for instant work
4	**vaseline**	— ointment used for burns, etc.
5	**zipper**	— a slide fastener for joining two pieces of cloth
6	**coke**	— Coca-cola, a soft drink
7	**pepsi**	— Pepsi-cola, another soft drink
8	**spumoni**	— Italian ice cream with chopped fruit and nuts
9	**cologne**	— perfumed bath water
10	**frigidaire**	— refrigerator for keeping foods, etc., cool

---

How did they get in? / **OUR LANGUAGE KEEPS GROWING**

Using the dictionary and other reference books to help you, write the definitions for 10 of these words used to name things in recent times.

cellophane	compact (car)
fiberglas	gremlin (space)
styrofoam	miniskirt
juke box	satellite
vinyl	fringe benefits (labor)
moon walk	stereo
feedback	gimmick
wetsuit	paperback
microfilm	walkie-talkie

What's the latest? / **KEEP YOUR LANGUAGE UP-TO-DATE**

Write the words that clearly fit the meaning suggested by the clues in parentheses to complete the sentences. All the answers appear in the previous lists.

1   While waiting for Dad to take him to the dentist, my brother took some __?__.

clue: *(pain relief tablets)*

2   So many things you buy nowadays come wrapped in __?__.

clue: *(a clear transparent paperlike product)*

3   Some airline pilots have reported seeing __?__ that cause engine troubles.

clue: *(mischievous unseen little creatures)*

4   When the magician pulls a flag out of a cigar, you know that he is using a __?__ to fool you.

clue: *(trick)*

5   After taking a shower, do you like to use a little __?__ to refresh your body?

clue: *(perfumed bath water)*

6   Youngsters are starting to make their own personal bookshelf by buying __?__.

clue: *(books with paper covers)*

7 How delightful it is to finish a good meal and then have some
__?__.

clue: *(Italian ice cream with fruits and nuts)*

8 One of the modern ways of dressing is to use a __?__ instead
of buttons on clothes.

clue: *(slide fastener)*

9 This modern __?__ can hold enough food and drink for a
family of four for several days.

clue: *(refrigerator)*

10 The whole world gazed in wonder as the astronauts started
on their __?__.

clue: *(treading the surface of the moon)*

Checkup quiz / **WORD ORIGINS**

Write the correct word or phrase that fits the meaning as expressed in the following sentences.

1 For good health, all milk has to be *(treated by a process that
kills bacteria)* for people to drink.

2 During the French Revolution, the angry peasants demanded
the nobles be *(beheaded)* publicly.

3 Surveys show the percentage of *(poisonous juice of tobacco)*
found in various brands of cigarettes.

4   Whenever a new ship is ready to go to sea, the owner or guest breaks a bottle of *(bubbly white wine)* against the hull.

5   My friend Angela can make a dress out of a piece of *(printed cloth)* that will make a fine present for my wife.

In This Lesson We Learned

Words have come into our language from several sources. Some come from the names of *people;* some from *places;* and others from *things.* Language is a living thing that grows with inventions, discoveries, etc.

FOREIGN
BORROWINGS

English is a mixture of many languages. During the past centuries, it has borrowed many words from other languages. Because of this, we have a great variety of words that we can use in speaking and writing.

English began as "Anglish" or the language spoken by the Anglo-Saxons who migrated to Britain from Germany. When the Danes and the Romans and later on the Normans conquered the British Isles, they left behind many new ideas to enrich the native speech of the Britons. Thus, we have a large number of foreign borrowings taken from Latin and French and the Scandinavian tongues. Commerce and industry brought additional words. Then, we received scientific words from the Greeks and quite a collection of words dealing with art, music, and painting from the Italians. We are still doing it. For example, the recent Webster dictionary includes the Japanese word for good-bye, "sayonara," as well as the Hawaiian "aloha," as a greeting.

Here are a few of the thousands of words we have borrowed in order to say whatever we want to say with a wider choice of expressions. Study this short list to get a taste of the foreign words, but always remember that there are many more for you to discover. Good luck! *Buona fortuna* (Italian)! *Buena suerte* (Spanish)! *Bonne chance* (French)!

252

Foreign Borrowings

LANGUAGES	WORDS NOW USED IN ENGLISH
SPANISH	adobe, burro, canyon, mesa, indigo
FRENCH	perfume, adieu, debutante, fiancée, cigarette
ITALIAN	pizza, macaroni, balcony, fresco, soprano
GERMAN	sauerkraut, frankfurter, waltz, strudel, ersatz
HEBREW	kosher, matzo, amen, cherub, kibbutz
LATIN	vitamin, chalice, mass, capital, dictionary
GREEK	biology, thermometer, anatomy, geography
CHINESE	tea, chow mein, chop suey, kumquat, pagoda
RUSSIAN	balalaika, steppes, tundra, samovar, tovarich
CELTIC	blarney, shamrock, whiskey, colleen, slogan
HINDI	bungalow, cashmere, jungle, loot, thug

OTHERS

Japanese	sayonara	**Arabic**	alcohol
Polish	mazurka	**Dutch**	skate
Turkish	coffee	**Mexican**	tamale
Hawaiian	aloha	**Norwegian**	fjord
Persian	chess	**Portuguese**	flamingo

Figure these out / **ENGLISH COMES FROM MANY LANGUAGES**

Can you figure out which foreign words given in the previous list fit the statements below? Use the clues (first and last letters) to help you spot the right words.

1 A deep valley with steep sides, often with a stream flowing

through it c—?—n

2 A copper urn used for heating water to make tea, used in

Russia and elsewhere s—?—r

253

3 Sweet talk full of flattery, or words used to persuade somebody   **b__?__y**

4 A platform with a railing projecting from a wall, or a gallery
upstairs in a theater   **b__?__y**

5 A chemical in food needed to keep you alive and free from
illness caused by poor diet   **v__?__n**

6 A delicious pastry made with apples, cheese, etc., and rolled
in a very thin layer of crispy dough   **s__?__l**

7 Things of value taken by force   **l__?__t**

8 A flat kind of cracker made out of flour without yeast, eaten
by Jewish people during Passover   **m__?__o**

9 A lively Polish dance in quick rhythm, especially at weddings
and parties   **m__?__a**

10 A game played by two persons, each with sixteen pieces on a
checkerboard, to capture or checkmate the opponent's king
(main piece)   **c__?__s**

Completion test / **FOREIGN BORROWINGS**

Write the foreign borrowed word that correctly fits the blank.
You will find the answers in the list on page 253.

1 The stringed instrument used to create the musical background for a Russian film is called a **b__?__a.**

2 Paris offers tourists an opportunity to purchase luxury items, such as Chanel 5 and other **p__?__s.**

3 The teen-age hunger may be satisfied with hamburgers, but more popular today is the tomato-and-cheese **p __?__ a.**

4 A small pack animal used in Arizona and Mexico is a donkey called a **b__?__o.**

5 The golden cup used to celebrate the mass in church is called a **c__?__ e.**

6 Chinese restaurants serve delicious foods and, as a special treat for dessert, sliced pineapple or some **k__?__s.**

7 When the doctor wants to test your body heat, he puts a **t__?__r** in your mouth under the tongue.

8 On St. Patrick's Day, it is customary for the Irish to wear a green **s__?__k** as a show of patriotism.

9 Dietary laws among the Orthodox Jews require the use of **k__?__r** foods.

10 Music for dancing written in three-quarter time was famous in old Vienna as the **w__?__z.**

Matching test / **FOREIGN BORROWINGS**

For each foreign word listed under Column *A*, write the letter of the correct meaning given under Column *B*. Check with your dictionary when in doubt.

A FOREIGN WORDS   B ENGLISH MEANINGS

1 bonus (Latin)   *a.* a woman's dressing gown

2 yacht (Dutch)   *b.* something extra given free

3 kimono (Japanese)   *c.* a color or dye

4 chrome (Greek)   *d.* a small ship used for pleasure

5 rodeo (Spanish)   *e.* an Irish accent in speech

6 brogue (Irish)   *f.* a roundup of cattle

7 moccasin (Indian)   *g.* chief silver coin of the Hebrews

8 delicatessen (German)   *h.* a piece of candy

9 bonbon (French)   *i.* a shoe made of soft leather

10 shekel (Hebrew)   *j.* a store selling cold cuts, etc.

In This Lesson We Learned

The English language began as an Anglo-Saxon branch of German. Now it contains thousands of foreign borrowings from many other languages.

Thousands of words float like ships from foreign ports carrying messages for us.

WORDS AS BRIDGES

Some words are bridges bringing people together: "I'm glad to meet you!" Some words are fences keeping people apart: "Don't bother me!" We are all sensitive to words of acceptance and words of rejection. Sometimes the right word makes beautiful music. Other times the wrong word feels like a dagger wound. Getting along with human beings depends largely on the way you behave toward them and the way you communicate with one another. Therefore:

> **Be careful to use language as a bridge or connection, not as a fence or barrier.**

The right words make friends / **PLEASANT AND UNPLEASANT WORDS AND EXPRESSIONS**

Here are some examples of the kinds of words we like to hear. Next to them are samples of expressions we don't like. Can you add five more to each list?

WORDS WE LIKE = BRIDGES	*WORDS WE DON'T LIKE =* FENCES
Please.	I, me, my, mine.
Thank you.	Do it yourself!

I love you.

Enclosed find check.

See you later.

Come over to my house.

Have another one.

Let's share the bill.

You're next.

Congratulations!

Get out of here!

It's your own fault.

No more left.

Give me_____!

Nobody home.

Put up or shut up!

You missed your chance.

Sorry.

Build bridges of communication / **WRITE SENTENCES
PLEASANT AND
UNPLEASANT**

Complete the following statements with words as bridges or fences, according to the meaning suggested (pleasant? unpleasant?).

1 I wish I could ...

2 How nice of you to send me such a surprise ...

3 If that's the way you feel about it, ...

4 Why did you have to ...

5 Oh, well, it really doesn't matter any more because ...

6 Thanks a lot for your help and ...

7 Let's get together again soon when ...

8 It's all right with me if you're in a hurry and ...

9 I hope you will feel better soon so that we two ...

10   You can tell that story to someone who ...

Build up your vocabulary / **BRIDGES OR FENCES?**

For each word below, write a pleasant synonym and an unpleasant antonym. Follow the sample.

	PLEASANT SYNONYM	UNPLEASANT ANTONYM
EXAMPLE: allow	permit	forbid
1 courage		
2 true		
3 busy		
4 friendly		
5 powerful		
6 generous		
7 joyous		
8 patient		

9 calm

10 cooperative

Be socially minded / **SHOW SENSITIVITY TO WORDS
AND EXPRESSIONS**

Label these expressions by writing **P** for **pleasant** or **U** for **unpleasant**. Your choice depends on the way we feel when someone else uses these words to us or about us!

1	Hello, Fatty.	*7*	Come as you are.
2	How tall you've grown.	*8*	This is a crumby joint.
3	You're always welcome.	*9*	I like your new skirt.
4	The tax is extra.	*10*	Who invited you?
5	It's raining again.	*11*	What's bugging you now?
6	You can count on me.	*12*	There's plenty more.

In This Lesson We Learned

Words are like *bridges* bringing people closer together; other words are like *fences* keeping them apart. We must be careful in using pleasant and unpleasant words because people are sensitive.

260

REVIEW TESTS IN VOCABULARY

There are three rules for success: try, try, try.

TEST I

Words carry over a certain feeling of *pleasure* or *displeasure* when we hear them. For example, if someone says, "Hey, stupid!" you feel insulted. But, if someone says, "I'm glad to know you!" you feel good. Read each expression listed below and tell whether it would make you feel good or bad if someone else said it to *you!* Why?

Expression

1 Keep out of this yard!

2 Come in; the water's fine.

3 I'm too busy now; wait outside.

4 Have a seat; I'll be right with you.

5 Stand in line; no talking!

6 Closed for the season.

7 Open for business.

8 You're a pain in the neck!

9 Thanks a lot for helping.

10 Use my bike if you like.

TEST II

Antonyms are words opposite in meaning. Write an antonym for each word below. Example: sweet / sour.

1	smiling	/	6	giant	/
2	tidy	/	7	damp	/
3	silent	/	8	working	/
4	prompt	/	9	shadow	/
5	merry	/	10	finished	/

TEST III

Synonyms are words having the same meaning. For example, refuse / reject. Select the correct synonym for each word in the left column.

1 **surprised** → eager, tearful, angry, amazed

2 **bold** → shy, daring, rough, surly

3 **sincere** → honest, deceitful, free, strong

4 **baffled** → tight, beaten, confused, weary

5 **timid** → brave, hardy, tiny, fearful

6 **dangerous** → clumsy, unsafe, slippery, powerful

7	**encourage**	$\rightarrow$	disapprove, invite, hearten, greet
8	**cautious**	$\rightarrow$	bewildered, slow, hasty, careful
9	**loneliness**	$\rightarrow$	terror, emptiness, singleness, company
10	**journey**	$\rightarrow$	trip, departure, arrival, location

TEST IV

Word backgrounds show how English words were borrowed from other languages or were based on names of people or places. For example, "spaghetti" comes from Italian; "pasteurized" comes from Pasteur.

For each word in Column *A*, write the letter of the matching item in Column *B*.

	A		*B*
1	hero	*a*	taken from Spanish; sweet potato
2	muslin	*b*	taken from Greek; man of courage
3	yam	*c*	taken from French; fine cotton fabric
4	memento	*d*	named after scientist Volta; electric power
5	tangerine	*e*	taken from Latin; reminder of the past
6	petite	*f*	named after inventor McAdam; road topping
7	Morris chair	*g*	named after Tangiers; reddish orange
8	volt	*h*	taken from French; small size
9	damask	*i*	named after inventor Morris; armchair with reclining back
10	macadam	*j*	named after Damascus; woven fabric

TEST V

Word elements *(prefixes, stems, suffixes)* make up our English words. You can figure out some meanings of words if you become acquainted with some common word elements used in everyday words. Here are 10 common prefixes. Can you tell the meaning of each word below?

1   *re* means "again"   rebuild, reprint, reproduce

2   *un* means "not"   unfair, unseen, unemployed

3   *dis* means "apart"   disappear, discourage, disarm

4   *in* means "not"   incomplete, inexpensive, inaccurate

5   *bi* means "twice"   biweekly, bicycle, binoculars

6   *trans* means "across"   transocean, transcontinental, transplant

7   *pre* means "before"   prepay, preschool, prefab

8   *non* means "not"   nonmetal, noncombat, nonunion

9   *anti* means "against"   antiwar, antislavery, antitrust

10 *sub* means "under"   submarine, subnormal, subcommittee

Be a builder.

INDEX